BEYOND GLOBALIZATION

"Today the most important thing, in my view, is to study the reasons why humankind does nothing to avert the threats about which it knows so much, and why it allows itself to be carried onward by some kind of perpetual motion. It cannot suffice to invent new machines, new regulations, new institutions. It is necessary to change and improve our understanding of the true purpose of what we are and what we do in the world. Only such a new understanding will allow us to develop new models of behavior, new scales of values and goals, and thereby invest the global regulations, treaties, and institutions with a new spirit and meaning."

President Vaclav Havel, Czech Republic

BEYOND GLOBALIZATION

Shaping a Sustainable Global Economy

Hazel Henderson

for the
New Economics Foundation
in association with
Focus on the Global South

KUMARIAN
PRESS

Beyond Globalization: Shaping a Sustainable Global Economy

Published 1999 in the United States of America by Kumarian Press, Inc.,
14 Oakwood Avenue, West Hartford, Connecticut 06119-2127 USA.

Production and design by The Sarov Press, Stratford, Connecticut.
The text of this book is set in Sabon 10/12.

Printed in Canada on acid-free paper containing post-consumer
waste by Transcontinental Printing and Graphics, Inc.
Text printed with vegetable oil-based ink.

∞The paper used in this publication meets the minimum requirements
of the American National Standard for Information Sciences—Permanence of
Paper for Printed Library Materials, ANSI Z39.48–1984.

Library of Congress Cataloging-in-Publication Data
Henderson, Hazel, 1933–
    Beyond globalization : shaping a sustainable global
economy / Hazel Henderson.
        p.   cm.
    Includes bibliographical references.
    ISBN 1–56549–107–6 (pbk. : alk. paper)
    1. International economic relations.   2. International economic
integration.   3. Competition, International.   I. Title.
HF1359.H458   1999
337—dc21   99–052716

08   07   06   05   04   03   02   01   00   10   9   8   7   6   5   4   3   2

First Printing 1999

CONTENTS

List of Illustrations   vi

1   Globalization: The Current Dilemmas   1

2   From Economics to Systems Thinking   10

3   Beyond Globalization   21

List of International Treaties   61

List of Charts   64

Selected Bibliography   72

Periodicals   77

Directory of Organizations   80

About the Author   89

New Economics Foundation   90

LIST OF ILLUSTRATIONS

Figure 1   Total Productive System of an
             Industrial Society   11

Figure 2   The Age of Light   14

Figure 3   Differing Models of Markets and Commons   18

Figure 4   Leading Edge Technologies Mimicking
             Nature   47

Figure 5   The New "Attention Economy"   54

Chart 1   The United Nations System   64

Chart 2   The Charter for Global Democracy:
             12 Areas for Urgent Action   65

Chart 3   A Canadian 10-Point Agenda:
             Meeting the Global Challenge to
             Eliminate Poverty   67

Chart 4   Menu of Policy Options for Global
             Financial Reform   69

GLOBALIZATION: THE CURRENT DILEMMAS

Globalization today involves the increasing interdependence of national economies, financial markets, trade, corporations, production, distribution, and consumer marketing. This globalization process is driven by two mainsprings. The first is technology which has accelerated innovation in telematics, computers, fiber optics, satellite, and other communications; their convergence with television, global multimedia, electronic bourses for trading stocks, bonds, currency, commodities, future options, and other derivatives; and the global explosion of e-commerce and the Internet. The second is the fifteen-year wave of deregulation, privatization, liberalization of capital flows, opening of national economies, extension of global trade, and the export-led growth policies that followed the collapse of the Bretton Woods fixed currency-exchange regime in the early 1970s. As the Soviet Union and its state-commanded economy crumbled, the wave of experimentation with deregulating global markets became known as "The Washington Consensus," that is: the dominant Western economic paradigm promoted by the United States (US), the World Bank, the International Monetary Fund (IMF), and their dominant schools of academic economists on both sides of the Atlantic.

Some economic historians have pointed to earlier thrusts toward globalization: from the fifteenth-century explorers of the Americas and the East Indies[1] to the open trade regimes in this century, which collapsed in the Great Depression of the 1930s and contributed to igniting World War II. Yet today, the evidence is in. Today's globalizations are new and are leading to the radical restructuring of national economies and societies. Spanish sociologist Manuel Castells' three-volume, *The Information Age: Economy, Society and Culture* (1998), is praised by many leading theorists, including Anthony Giddens of the London School of Economics as "the most compelling attempt yet made to map the contours of the global information age." Castells states: "A new world is taking shape in this end of millennium. It originated in the historical coincidence around the late 1960s and mid-1970s of three independent processes, the information technology revolution, the economic crisis of both capitalism and statism, and their subsequent restructuring; and the blooming of cultural social movements, such as libertarianism, human rights, feminism, and environmentalism . . . the interactions between these processes and the reactions they triggered brought into being a new dominant social structure, the network society . . . and the new informational/global economy and a new culture."[2]

Real or Unreal—The Economy Today

With today's globalization of finance in cyberspace, key cities such as London, New York, Tokyo, Singapore, Hong Kong, Frankfurt, and Sao Paulo have become expressions of this new global, networked information-based economy. Finance, which is supposed to serve the world's real production and exchange processes, has largely de-coupled from the "bricks and mortar" of real economies of local places and communities. Today's globalized economy has led to a sixteen-fold increase in world trade since World War II, worth over US$4 trillion per year (some 15 to 20 percent of measured global GDP). More than forty thousand multinational companies with twenty-five thousand foreign affiliates dominate this two-thirds of global trade. Yet this huge volume of trade accounts for less than 10 percent of the twenty-four-hour global currency trading of US$1.5 trillion every *day*.

This global economy of flows in these market networks is increasingly abstract and divorced from national policy-makers and local affairs, grassroots lives and livelihoods as well as the natural ecosystem. This has triggered new risks and new inequalities. These include the further marginalization of social groups, indigenous peoples, and whole countries, such as many in Africa; widening gaps between rich and poor; the new division between "info-rich" and "info-poor" and an overall increase in global poverty, as documented in successive editions of the UNDP *Human Development Report*. Within one generation, according to the Living Planet Index assembled by the World Wide Fund for Nature and the New Economics Foundation, around 30 percent of Nature's productive capacity has been lost.

Real Issues and Real Problems

Today, ever more problems and issues have become global—beyond the reach of national governments: from climate change, cross-border pollution, desertification, and loss of bio-diversity to space junk. Proliferating weapons-trafficking, drugs trading, organized crime, nuclear and toxic wastes and epidemics spread by air travel, not to mention global terrorism, cannot be addressed by any nation acting alone. Overall profits of global crime networks in 1994 were estimated at US$750 billion to US$1 trillion. Some US$500 billion is laundered into the global financial markets.[3] Powerful new biotechnologies such as: cloning and genetically modified organisms require international safety-testing and standards. Meanwhile, dealing with refugees, migrant populations, displaced people, and the continued growth of mega-cities—while maintaining safety-nets—requires massive public investments. Reactions to globalization, and to "Western" technologies and ideas have included rising fundamentalism (Christian in the USA, Muslim in many countries) and new searches for identity in ethnicity or nationalism—and the conflicts these often engender.

Nations face all these problems at the same time that their tax revenues are eroding: diverted into tax havens or Swiss banks. Powerful special interests lobby in most countries for tax favors—undermining the redistributive role of taxation. The tax bases of municipalities and local governments are also eroding as Internet-based e-commerce outflanks stores on high streets. In the US, state governors and city mayors warn President Clinton that his "no taxing of e-commerce" policy is driving local merchants out of business. Local commerce must pay property taxes, collect sales taxes—which in turn support local schools, hospitals, fire, and police—which e-commerce does not. Indeed, the explosive growth of Internet e-commerce is based on this tax-subsidy and cheap access to telecommunications systems which has resulted in a stock market bubble. Money itself has morphed into information, as debit cards, credit cards, and trillions of digitized bits flow between millions of computers.

All these new problems and issues are driving national governments into pooling or sharing their sovereignty to set up or strengthen international agencies, rule-making bodies, and global standards. The most prominent example of sovereignty-sharing is the European Union. Power-sharing has not come easily, but operates effectively within the principle of subsidiarity: control retained at local or provincial levels where appropriate.

Positive Potentials of Globalization

There is also much good news brought by the globalization of the new networked information economy. Along with today's trashiest television, movies, Internet porn, and video games comes distance-learning and college courses for people confined to their homes, prisoners, and semi-skilled employees seeking new careers. The networked society has advanced democracy worldwide, helped tumble dictators, opened up repressive regimes, advanced pluralism, and human rights and sped the end of the Cold War. Most noticeable has been the advance of citizen organizations and movements—now a distinct "third sector" in the world holding the private and public sectors more accountable. More access to information has helped empower citizens, consumer choice, employees, and socially responsible investors. The information society has created new winners—and morphed into an "age of truth." Corporations are learning that "green-washing" does not work for long. Politicians find themselves more accountable for shady dealing and dubious contributions to their election campaigns. Grassroots citizens' campaigns can go global as with Jubilee 2000—now in forty countries—which has changed the thinking of governments, central banks, and economists about the need to cancel un-repayable and illegitimate debts of the poorest countries. A new identity is emerging: the global citizen; even before the arrival of global governance structures.

Other positive aspects of today's uneven globalization are the rapid proliferation and sharing of concepts of sustainable development, commonly defined as development which meets the needs of the present without compromising the ability of future generations to meet their own needs. Innovative ideas for greener technologies, local sustainability, homegrown economies, community-contract organic agriculture, local currencies, and barter systems, micro-credit, and new indicators beyond GNP are all transmitted at web-speed. Never has it been easier to share visions of re-shaping our societies and global economy on principles of social justice, citizen participation and ecological awareness.

The Unreal Economy: Our Global Casino

The Asian economic meltdown has led to massive coverage on its causes. Early explanations, from the old paradigm of the Washington Consensus, focused on domestic deficiencies of Asian countries, rather than shortcomings in private markets. The 1999 rebound of these Asian economies (largely via deficit spending) has fueled Western markets—and a new complacency. But the continual shocks and instabilities in today's global financial markets have finally led to some cautious re-thinking on the part of finance ministers and central bankers on the need for a "new financial architecture." Ever since the collapse of the Bretton Woods system in 1971, the global financial system has been characterized by increasing turbulence, mounting debt, and a de-coupling of finance and currency flows from the real world economies of production, trade, and consumption that money is supposed to facilitate and measure. While free market theory is that investment should be allowed to flow where it can be put to best use, the current set-up does not allow this happen. A quick return takes priority over longer-term investment. If a country took the same attitude to its investment, it would put no resources into education . . . clearly not a very secure strategy.

International financial operations escape national regulations and are centered in London, New York, Tokyo, Hong Kong, Singapore, and off-shore tax havens: Switzerland, the Cayman Islands, the British Virgin Islands, Cyprus, Antigua, Liechtenstein, Panama, the Netherlands Antilles, the Bahamas, Luxembourg, and the Channel Islands. More than twenty thousand corporations are chartered in the Cayman Islands and the deposits in its 575 chartered banks now total some $500 billion. Only 106 of these banks have a physical presence in Cayman and an estimated 1.5 million of such corporations now operate "offshore" in secrecy—up from 200,000 in the late 1980s. Americans account for some 40 percent of these assets.[4] The world's secretive private banking services (for clients with over $1 million) have risen from $4.3 trillion in 1986 to $10 trillion in 1997 and projecting $13.6 trillion by 2000. The largest players are Union Bank of Switzerland ($580 billion), Credit Suisse ($290 billion), and in the US; Citibank, Chase, and Merrill Lynch (with $100 billion each).

Meanwhile, the deflationary effect of the Asian meltdown is still lurking and may yet be felt in the world economy. In the US, while trade deficits are huge (in recent years averaging US$20 billion per month), private corporate debt is exploding, corporate bond defaults reached 5 percent, and consumer debt is ballooning, while savings rates are negative.[5] The US and European stock markets are still pumped up with billions in flight capital seeking safer havens, as well as huge increases of borrowing (at 50 percent margins) for stock purchases on Wall Street. Weak banking sectors, especially in Japan, have engaged in mega-mergers that may not make them stronger. A fast positive feedback loop is created by the "herd behavior" of asset managers who follow asset allocation theory and feel obliged to buy the big indexes: Dow Jones, Standard and Poor's, NASDAQ, and London's FTSE100. This herd behavior effect is reinforced in the US by the "prudent man rule," which prevents asset managers from straying far beyond such blue chip stocks—thereby bidding up the big indexes and better described as "the prudent lemming rule."

Unreal Accounting

The truth is that it is not hard to make such forms of globalization look good if your accounting disenfranchises a significant minority, ignores the running down of natural resources, and discounts future risks.

We measure according to our dominant cultural view of what is valuable. When GNP/GDP accounts were set up in World War II, bombs, bullets, and war production were the goal, while the value of children, a healthy educated citizenry, infrastructure, social safety nets, and the environment were all set at zero. This statistical viewpoint is still perpetuated—not only by bureaucratic inertia but by the sectors, interest groups, and politically powerful forces which benefit from such a system of national accounts. Military budgets remain off-limits while social safety nets, health, education, environment, and even repairs to infrastructure are pushed down national budget priority lists. Employment, caring work, parenting, social services, and safety-nets have been slowly devalued while finance itself (i.e., paper asset-shuffling) is over valued. The financial services sectors have grown ninefold—out of all proportion to those real economies of "Main Street" they were designed to track and serve.[6] This same process has also devalued the commodities sector and natural resources, currently at a twelve-year low. One could simply make more money by holding and trading financial assets.

Global Electronic Commerce

Many critics like myself pointed out over the past twenty-five years that this overblown finance sector was a "bubble" and when it deflated, as on October 19, 1987, that the world's traditional resource and human-capital based economies of the world would actually benefit.[7] Even though cyber-libertarians, Internet entrepreneurs, and electronic currency traders do not like earthbound constraints, the laws of thermodynamics still operate. One cannot fill a car's gas tank with a "virtual gallon of petrol" or drive across the "flow of services" of a bridge. All this was pointed out by Nicholas Georgescu-Roegen in his *The Entropy Law and the Economic Process* in 1971, whom I have regarded as the much sought-after "new Keynes."[8]

Although improvements in communications and materials sciences have since led to a profound de-materializing of OECD economies, today's debates involve the extent to which, this process—which futurist Buckminster Fuller called "ephemeralization," can continue substituting services, recycling, knowledge, and communications for natural resources. The Wuppertal Institute (Germany) and the Rocky Mountain Institute (US) have studied these processes and estimate between four-fold and ten-fold efficiency increases in energy and materials use are possible (see Directory). Here is where investments in people and social infrastructure are key. Societies cannot continue de-materializing their economies without investing in maintaining such social architecture and human capital for further advances in research.[9] Knowledge, human capital, trust, cohesive values, and sound management of the planet's biodiversity and natural resources are now the key factors of production. Yet paradoxically, the current shape of the global information economy and e-commerce starves governments (national and local) of the tax resources needed to invest in human resources and new infrastructure.

Today, globalizing electronic markets offer a "fast-forward" view of what we can expect. Over half of *Business Week*'s one hundred biggest global corporations in 1999 are in information and financial services. They accelerate the dominance of the below-full-cost price system (today's prices do not include social and environmental costs) over diverse traditional values, cultures, and institutions, which form the "cultural DNA codes" of different societies. Thus they promote lower prices as a boon to consumers, while the costs pile up unnoticed or get paid by someone else. Adequate domestic macro-economic policies and investments in public services infrastructure fall victim to volatile unregulated markets and the global financial bubble.

Governments Are Still Responsible

All this does not mean that governments are powerless.[10] Yet we still see national governments and politicians ducking these responsibilities, which are often part of their electoral promises to voters. Even the most democratically elected politicians too often renege on these promises and begin to cast their policies in line with the status quo and special interests. Money has become the curse of democratic political processes in many OECD and developing countries aspiring to become more democratic. For example, Mexican contributions of US$40 million to US Congress members helped to narrowly pass the NAFTA vote. Many recent surveys find that only 30 percent of Americans trust Washington politicians and public officials.[11]

In Europe and elsewhere, many other scandal-ridden governments put their taxpayers' funds on the global auction block, along with their workforces and natural and environmental resources, in the new global bidding war to lure (bribe) corporations, banks, and financial institutions to locate in their countries. These bidding wars broker taxpayers' funds to subsidize such new corporate facilities, often at absurd costs. For example, London-based *The Economist* reported (February 1, 1997, p. 25) that in 1991 Portugal paid Auto Europa, Ford, and Volkswagen $254,000 per job created, while the state of Alabama, USA, "bribed" Mercedes-Benz with $167,000 per job created. These enormous corporate subsidies might have financed micro-businesses or provided guaranteed incomes for life to many of these prospective job holders[12].

Cronyism is endemic—not something recently discovered in Asia. Heads of state troop dutifully to the World Economic Forum in Davos to offer these deregulation "sweeteners," subsidies, and tax breaks to corporate chief executives. They bargain away their citizens' taxes and sovereignty in the now-familiar global "race-to-the-bottom." *The Economist*'s Clive Crook tells us that governments are not in retreat but getting bigger citing percentages of GNPs spent by governments. These overall figures do not tell us how much of this government spending is steered by financial and corporate interests into the billions of tax favors and annual subsidies they enjoy. Indeed, many governments have become corporate "cash cows" while some have sunk into "kleptocracies."

Global Corporations

Corporate law allows companies to limit their liabilities and evade public accountability. Worse, in the US, corporate charters, granted by government, allow them all the rights of "natural persons." These corporate and financial entities have grown over the years to wield enormous power over elected and governmental officials. Waves of mega-mergers are increasing monopolistic power in many sectors. At the same time, management of the corporations is moving into cyberspace. Michael Dell, CEO of Dell Computers exults "management, ever more reliant on information will soon migrate to the ether. Physical infra-structures are becoming obsolete."[13] Citizens in most OECD countries are organizing for government protection from corporate irresponsibility.

An example was the proposal championed by corporations for a Multilateral Agreement on Investment (MAI). Over years, step by step, agreement by agreement, states had negotiated UN protocols on biodiversity, climate change, and fifty years of treaties on standards around human and employee rights and environmental protection. Some 560 civic groups from sixty-eight countries around the world managed to derail the Multilateral Agreement on Investment (MAI), which would have undermined these existing protocols in order to favor corporations over citizens. The same concerns are now driving the global campaign to stop or redirect the WTO Millennium Round.

Needed: An Accounting Revolution

Wall Street hype promises information-sector led productivity and globalization will usher in a promised land of steady GNP-growth, low inflation, and unprecedented wealth. In September 1999, *Wired*, the magazine of the Internet sector, foresaw a Dow Jones average at 30,000 in four years, while the staid *Atlantic Monthly*'s lead article seriously argued that the Dow should reach 36,000. A more realistic view is that global capital flight to Wall Street and other factors are driving a classic bubble. Still other scenarios set local, ethnic, community, and nationalistic backlashes against the backdrop of globalization.[14] The reality is that each of these hypotheses stem from different paradigms and interpretations, which will produce conflicting forecasts. The only way forward is to go beyond the limited tools of economic measurement that we are using and develop a more sophisticated approach to understand the global system we are creating.

Notes

1. See, for example, D. Landes, *The Wealth and Poverty of Nations* (New York: W.W. Norton, 1998) for an important interpretation of economic development which embraces culture, climate, and geography.
2. M. Castells, *The Information Age: Economy, Society and Culture* (Malden, Mass. and Oxford: Blackwell, 1998), Vol III, p. 356.
3. M. Castells, p. 169.
4. R. Morgenthau, "On the Trail of Global Capital," *New York Times*, November 9, 1998, p. 125.
5. "A Time Bomb for Borrowers?" *Business Week*, August 30, 1999, p. 30 and "The Default Dilemma," *Business Week*, September 6, 1999, p. 72.
6. P. Dembinski and Schoenenberger, "The Safe Landing of the Financial Balloon Is Not Impossible," *Finance & the Common Good* (Autumn 1998), Geneva.
7. *UTNE Reader*, August 1997
8. See my review in *Harvard Business Review* (1971).
9. See, for example, D. Lamberton, ed. *The Economies of Information and Knowledge* (New York: Penguin Books, 1971).

10. See, for example, L. Weiss, (1998) *The Myth of the Powerless State*, Cornell University Press.
11. A.F. Kay, "Locating Consensus for Democracy," Americans Talk Issues Foundation, 1998.
12. As documented, for example, in "What Corporate Welfare Costs," *Time* (November 1998). Website: www.time.com.
13. "The World in 1999 Supplement," *The Economist*, p. 96.
14. See, for example, J. Ørstrom Møller, *The Future European Model* (Westport, Conn.: Praeger/Greenwood, 1995) and S. Huntington, "Clash of Civilizations," *Foreign Affairs* 72, No. 3 (Summer 1993).

2

FROM ECONOMICS TO SYSTEMS THINKING

I have detailed elsewhere the gulf between today's economic globalization and economics theories and textbooks with their assumptions of "efficient markets," general economic equilibrium, and "rational" actors in markets with perfect information all operating with negligible impacts on innocent bystanders and the environment.[1] This theoretical lag has played a key role in justifying the existing system and entrapping millions in poverty, unemployment, under-employment, and in the loss of previously self-reliant livelihoods.

Some of the statistical work is underway—from re-tooling GNP/GDP to account for natural and human capital, and subtracting social and environmental costs to re-calculate Consumer Price Indexes (CPIs).

Understanding Wealth Creation

It is now imperative for example that national accounts in all countries and the United Nations System of National Accounts (UNSNA) include caring unpaid work to maintain traditional livelihoods, family, and community life. These changes have been recommended since World War II by myself and a minority of economists: K. W. Kapp (1950); E. J. Mishan (1974); K. W. Boulding (1968); B. Ward (1962), and by the New Economics Foundation (NEF) and increasing numbers of economists. The UNSNA was set up in the 1950s after being designed originally to maximize war production in the United Kingdom during World War II. In 1995 the United Nations Human Development Program (UNDP) produced an estimate of $16 trillion of such unpaid caring volunteer work, simply missing from 1995 global GDP of $24 trillion[2]—illustrating the enormity of this omission.

Such unpaid work (parenting, caring for old and sick family members, growing food for family and community needs, maintaining households, volunteering in community service, do-it-yourself home and community construction, and repair projects) is estimated as some 50 percent of all production in OECD countries and some 60 to 65 percent in developing countries—depending on the size of their traditional village-based and indigenous economies.[3]

Figure 1

Total Productive System of an Industrial Society

(Three-Layer Cake with Icing)

GNP-Monetized
1/2 of Cake

Top two layers
Monetized, officially measured GNP generates all economic statistics (15% "underground" illegal, tax-dodging)

Non-Monetized
Productive 1/2 of Cake

Lower two layers
Non-monetized altruism, sharing "caring economy" subsidizes top two GNP-cash sectors with unpaid labor and environmental costs absorbed or unaccounted, risks passed to future generations

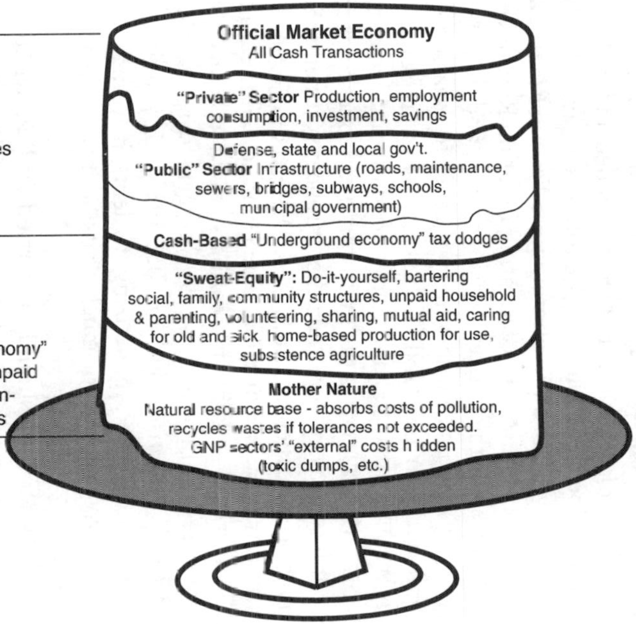

Official Market Economy
All Cash Transactions
"Private" Sector Production, employment consumption, investment, savings
Defense, state and local gov't.
"Public" Sector Infrastructure (roads, maintenance, sewers, bridges, subways, schools, muncipal government)
Cash-Based "Underground economy" tax dodges
"Sweat-Equity": Do-it-yourself, bartering social, family, community structures, unpaid household & parenting, volunteering, sharing, mutual aid, caring for old and sick home-based production for use, subsistence agriculture
Mother Nature
Natural resource base - absorbs costs of pollution, recycles wastes if tolerances not exceeded. GNP sectors' "external" costs hidden (toxic dumps, etc.)

GNP "Private" Sector rests on
↓
GNP "Public" Sector which rests on
↓
Social Cooperative Caring Economy which rests on
↓
Nature's Layer

Source: Hazel Henderson, *Paradigms in Progress* (San Francisco: Berrett-Koehler Publishers, 1991).

The environmentalists' critique of the UNSNA has also been insistent. Many "green GDP" alternatives have been proposed such as PQLI (Physical Quality of Life Index) by David Morris[4], the (ISEW) Index of Sustainable Economic Welfare of Herman Daly and John Cobb[5] now calculated in many versions in OECD countries including the US, UK, and Sweden, and many others.

Macro-economic policies should also account for the valuable public goods and services that add to quality of life but are unpriced (e.g., police and fire services, infrastructure, health and environmental protection agencies, etc.), without which complex technological economies cannot function. Thus, the US CPI may be overstated by as much 1.5 percent, as the US Boskin Commission says, or by more than this if the value of unpriced public services are factored in. Energy and food prices continue to be excluded from the "core" rate—along with depreciation of infrastructure and other national assets. *The Economist* sensibly recommended adding financial and real estate asset inflation to Consumer Price Indexes (May 9, 1998). All this statistical revisioning will end up recalibrating US Federal Reserve and other central bank policies and the Non Accelerating Inflation Rate of Unemployment (NAIRU), as well as the budget, social security, and deficits.

More than ever, new multi-disciplinary metrics to measure quality of life must supplement current GNP/GDP systems of national accounts (UNSNAs), to account for social and human capital and ecological assets and unpaid work. Most urgent is the inclusion of an asset budget so as to properly account for infrastructure and other public investments. Such huge investments have been "expensed" in GNP/GDP—leading to massive budget "deficits" and overstating inflation. The US followed the lead of New Zealand and Switzerland in 1996 in creating such an asset account for its public infrastructure—leading to its 1999 budget "surplus." With even London-based *The Economist* (October 10, 1998, p. 18) calling for Japan to start "printing money" (i.e., monetizing its debt), it would surely make more sense to properly account for much of its "debt" as the public assets which it financed.

These public investments should be carried and expensed over their useful life, often fifty to one hundred years. GNP/GDP is a "cash-flow" statement of money-dominated transactions, with such longer-term investments (infrastructure, education, infant health, etc.) treated as "consumption" and written off each year. Try running a corporation that way—as if a costly productive facility could not be amortized over its useful life. This statistical correction reduced the US budget deficit by approximately $100 billion per year, by accounting for some infrastructure assets, but still not education or other investments in human or social capital (e.g., science, research and development, etc.). The US's budget surplus was also achieved by additional tax collected on Wall Street gains and some $100 billion reduction in still-bloated military expenditures.

This budget "surplus," claimed to be the result of superior economic management (certainly improved accounting) attracted billions in flight capital from other jittery markets after Asia's meltdown went global, seeking safe havens in the US stock and bond markets. If all other countries simply made the same re-calculations to their own GDPs, all would soon show similar budget "surpluses." So why don't they? Surely, such sensible corrections to all national accounts are preferable to the moral hazards of putting taxpayers at further risk of bailing out speculators again, as proposed by *Business Week* in "a global write-down of debt" (i.e., private debt) in its editorial of September 7, 1998.

European Union member countries (with an average of 11 percent unemployment) have cut their domestic safety-nets to attain the Maastricht criteria which included 3 percent or less of budget-deficits. Some years ago, I urged that the Commission's policy staff might check their member nations' GDPs for asset accounts to see if public infrastructure investments were missing. This might have saved painful budget cuts and the ensuing political unrest and strikes—particularly in France. The new euro, overseen by the independent European Central Bank (ECB) will constrain domestic economic policies further—exacerbated by the "growth and stability pact." Further straitjacketing of fiscal policies will force de-regulation and cuts in employment security and benefits for employees in the eleven euro countries and will promote "labor mobility" between them (i.e., more economic migration with its social costs unaccounted). At the same time, in the current global economic crisis, a great proportion of public debt in Japan, Korea, other Asian countries, as well as in Europe and Latin America could be reduced along with unemployment by such accounting corrections.[6] It must be emphasized that such asset accounts in GDP should also includes investments in long term social capital (education, health, child development, and research and development) to maintain a society's knowledge-base and general quality of life. The World Bank's new Wealth Index, introduced in 1995, moves in the right direction—but still has little effect on operations.

Meanwhile, the UNSNA still over-values the goods and artifacts of the receding industrial era, while many OECD economies are approaching the US's 70 percent of services. Such services, however, still do not include those of the unpaid informal and household economies. These sectors are eroding daily through neglect—in broken families, community breakdown, drugs, inner-city decay, and spreading epidemics such as tuberculosis. Statisticians in the US are at work overhauling the categories of GNP/GDP, which still are dominated by widgets and goods, to include software, services, knowledge industries and intellectual capital. Similarly, accounting firms are grappling with "intellectual capital" and "good will" in corporate balance sheets overhauls including social, environmental, and ethical auditing —representing the biggest advance in accounting since the invention of double-entry bookkeeping. But the conceptual confusion continues as we proceed further into the "Age of Light" (see Figure 2) based on deeper knowledge of nature, ourselves, and powered by renewable resources and solar energy.[7] Before we steer our economic policies back toward the common good, quality of life, and sound environmental management—we must complete this accounting revolution.

Figure 2
The Age of Light
Emerging Lightwave Technologies (Photonics)

- Fiber optics — ...communications cabling, voice, data, etc.
- Optical scanners — ...supermarkets, banks, on-line computer systems
- Lasers — ...laser surgery, laser printers, laser phonographs turntables, laser bottles to see atoms, laser propulsion, Star Wars laser weapons systems, laser art
- Holography — ...computer assisted design (CAD), computer assisted manufacturing (CAM), computer integrated manufacturing (CIM), art
- Solar technologies — ...passive solar heating and cooling, Trombe walls, solar thermal energy conversion, ocean thermal, tidal and wave power, bio-energy conversion, hydroponics, aquaculture, solar reflector "power towers," photochemical conversion (artificial and natural photosynthesis), photovoltaics, solar cell arrays for powering satellites, space-based solar collectors, solar sails for deep space voyages
- Optical computers — ...use light pulses instead of electrical impulses - pushing toward the speed of light
- Multiprocessor, parallel computers, and neural net computers — ...very fast architecture allows simultaneous, rather than sequential processing, speech and voice recognition, language and artificial intelligence (AI) applications
- Imaging technologies — ...TV images, liquid crystal screens, magnetic imaging diagnostics
- Biotechnologies — ...gene splicing, designing, molecular engineering, medical diagnostics, immunology, tissue culture, cloning, plant hybridization and "re-designing," and bio-remediation
- Gene machines — ...which automate the synthetic assembly of genes
- DNA sequencers — ...which "speed read" the DNA code in cells
- Tagging & tracking chemicals & genes — ...using luciferase, etc.
- Nano technologies — ...molecular "machines" to assemble, repair molecules, in many diverse ways (e.g., theories of Eric Drexler in *Engines of Creation*, 1986)

Photons (sunlight) falling on the earth supply enough energy in
10 minutes to put our entire five billion population in orbit!

Source: Adapted from Hazel Henderson, *Paradigms in Progress* (San Francisco: Berrett-Koehler Publishers, 1991).

Systems Thinking

The complexities of understanding the new global economy require going beyond economics to a multi-disciplinary approach. In *Economics: The Culture of a Controversial Science* (1998), University of Chicago Business School Professor Melvin W. Reder describes today's "crisis within economics": the insecurity of the discipline's status, the internal disagreements on its scope and methods—and whether economics is a science or "disguised ideology."[8] Researchers linked to organizations such as the New Economics Foundation, including myself, James Robertson, Simon Zadek, Ann Pettigrew, and others outside mainstream economics have engaged for many years in this re-thinking of economics. Addressing the tasks of restructuring the global economy requires a multitude of disciplines and metrics beyond money—that is, a systems approach.

Systems thinking was born in this century precisely to embrace the complexities of institutional change and the dynamic behavior of large organizations and global systems. The inter-related tasks for reshaping the global economy are at seven levels: global, international, national, corporate, local governments, civic society, and the family/individual. This is necessary for mapping coherent strategies at each level, analysing how they interact and how they can reinforce each other. Systems theorists have shown that many of our social and environmental problems experienced at one level are generated at another level. The reductionist paradigm of solving problems, one at a time, in isolation, without an overview of the whole system is precisely what generates impacts elsewhere: that is, the law of unintended consequences.

The planet teaches us these systems lessons every day and nature endowed humans with big brains (most of whose capacity is unused). We have mental toolboxes to detect patterns and whole paradigms and the ability to focus in on detail. To comprehend the global economy we need to use our mental "cameras" both to pull back and take "wide shots" and to zoom in and focus—at all these seven levels. Another mental tool of systems thinking is to look for feedback loops. These are the pathways along which actions and impacts are transmitted. These feedbacks are termed "positive" if the feedback loop amplifies the effect (e.g., humans have children who then have more children—so that today, the human population on the planet has increased to today's six billion). Feedbacks are termed "negative" if they damp down or cancel out the effects of actions (e.g., if human values change and people have fewer children, fertility rates drop as they have in forty countries today). Watching for these feedback loops is essential to mapping how networks and human organizations work and interact—as well as to find optimal policies and intervention points.[9]

Our global networked economy is composed of millions of daily actions and interactions at all levels—between governments, banks, investors, corporations, employees, and consumers—all nested in ecosystems. Sadly, many millions are increasingly left out of these networks. These include the poor, indigenous peoples, and the unemployed, and those in traditional informal sectors, use-value agriculture, and unpaid home-based activities in villages worldwide. Almost the entire continent of Africa (except for South Africa) has been bypassed by the flows of the global economy as described by Yash Tandon.[10] Inner cities and rural areas in many OECD countries are similarly bypassed. Feedback signals on their plight are weak. In the US, the Boston-based citizens group United for a Fair Economy documents the polarization of the US economy. For example, just 7.8 percent of the 1997–98 *increase* in the wealth of the four hundred richest Americans (US$7.8 billion) would provide Headstart pre-schooling for two-thirds of the poor children still unserved.[11] Even in the rich countries, wealth, power, and information have migrated into the global fast lane.

The Bankruptcy of Conventional Economics

In this way, systems thinkers and futurists contend that most economic models in the public and private sector take us into the future with eyes fixed on the rear-view mirror. Many excellent books listed in the bibliography offer corrective analyses and broader perspectives on alternative paths to sustainability. Meanwhile, most economic textbooks still see human beings as either the guinea pigs in the computer models of fashionable social simulators or as the atoms of traditional Newtonian physics. This "objective" view (which *does* make the mathematics easier!) assumes that all human actions in society are irrelevant, statistically damped out by the Law of Large Numbers. Even powerful producers are assumed to have no impact on the structure of the economy in models. Some economists and most systems thinkers are of the opposite opinion, believing that financial markets are influenced by large institutions—from governments to global corporations and institutional investors—in increasingly interwoven global real-time networks, where over-shoots and herd behavior are amplified. Thus, game theory, chaos models, anthropology, and psychology become sharper tools for examining how markets are affected by the interactions of mutual expectations of players. Unfortunately, the "Artificial Society"—models of mathematical economists often program their simulated "human agents" with the same competitive, self-maximizing, economic behavior as institutions—and, unsurprisingly, recreate poverty gaps and trade wars.[12] The now defrocked "quants" and "rocket scientists" whose computer models calculate risk factors and the prices of derivatives allow a 20 to 40 percent risk factor. They have still led to huge losses. The red-faced Nobel Committee which awarded the 1997 economics prize to the two partners of the ill-fated Long Term Capital Management hedge fund, awarded the 1998 prize to Amartya Sen, who studies poverty and moral issues.

A few innovative economists (borrowing models from systems and game theory and from chaos and complex adaptive systems studies) have moved beyond the Industrial Age, mechanistic worldview. For example, the Santa Fe Institute's W. Brian Arthur uses fifty-year-old cybernetic, feedback driven systems models to illustrate that in network markets there are increasing (not diminishing) returns to scale and "path-dependency" in innovation (i.e., initial conditions will amplify in non-linear systems due to positive feedbacks).[13] This phenomenon underlies the rush to colonize the Internet by e-commerce, startup ventures, and Microsoft's market domination. These new "dot com" companies rack up huge debts to rapidly capture market share. Ecologists study similar "colonization" strategies of fast growing annual plants and weeds. As Internet investors are re-learning, hundreds of early-stage "weeds" get shaken out as new technology sectors mature—in the process Schumpeter first described as "the creative destruction" of capitalism. Stanford University's Paul Romer in the US and Demos' Charles Leadbeater in the UK remind economists of what futurists have known for decades: that technology must be incorporated as a key variable in all macro-economic models. Technology and knowledge, far from being "residual" factors in productivity are clearly driving forces. Yet "productivity" measures are also hotly debated; Robert Gordon sees two-thirds of US productivity since 1995 as the result of statistical revisions.[14] Michael Rothschild, in *Bionomics* (1990), and Kevin Kelly in *Out of Control* (1994), re-vision economies as ecosystems in terms long familiar to futurists and ecologists, echoing my *Creating Alternative Futures: The End of Economics* (1978, 1996). Clearly, interdisciplinary dialogues between all these worldviews are now urgently needed. In this way sharper analytical tools and better policy proposals may emerge.

These arguments underlie today's debate in the financial press about the nature of the "New Economy," the role of millions of independent day traders and the explosive US stock market rises and volatility. All this is key to whether US Federal Reserve Board Chairman Alan Greenspan's new view of the statistical lag in measuring productivity is correct. The US "surplus," wildly overestimated to reach US$6 trillion by 2015, triggered a new debate over cutting taxes or even paying down the national debt to lower interest rates. The enthusiasts hail the transition from industrialism to a global information economy. *Business Week* has frequently editorialized that globalization, and the increasing competition it brings, *does* discipline even the biggest firm's pricing—just as it does wages. This echoes calls for dumping the Phillips Curve, the supposed trade-off between inflation and unemployment, as I have urged since 1978. (Even Phillips, a UK economist extrapolating from scanty data in the 1950s didn't believe in the Phillips Curve.) As a result, the NAIRU has been shifted into lower territory so that interest rates *can* be reduced and sustainable economic growth can proceed, with fuller employment, in a new virtuous cycle.

All this sounds great and it is half-right, as a market "cash flow model" (i.e., the conventional monetarist "bathtub" model of the national economy as a hydraulic system). But it overlooks structural factors, such as over-capacity and debt and the need to secure global public goods. The real "New Economy" we need has to be more than this.

In the UK, Roger Bootle makes a related case in his *The Death of Inflation* (1996,1997) but with a longer time scale interpretation beyond simple monetarism. Bootle's more radical conclusion is that OECD economies face a future of deflation. Alternative economists would term this under-consumption and lack of purchasing power among the poor (who would spend, not save money). This is why many, including myself, James Robertson, Robert Theobald, and others recommend tax-reform to include a "citizens wage" or guaranteed income. Other necessary reforms include broadening capital ownership, as pioneered by Louis and Patricia Kelso, myself, Jeff Gates, Shann Turnbull, Genevieve Vaughan, and others.

Furthermore, most economists still work for private sector banks, financial institutions, corporations or government agencies. They bestride the policy process offering concepts for managing global commons (e.g., ocean fish stocks and biodiversity) based on extending property rights. They bring along their obsolete models of Pareto Optimality (which assumes away unequal distribution of wealth, power, and information). Economists propose to enclose the last commons as "property regimes" for economic efficiency while omitting the truth that all such schemes, including pollution permits and emissions trading, are essentially *political* allocations of resources. Futurists and systems theorists see the commons as closed systems requiring win-win rules (see Figure 3, "Differing Models of Markets and Commons"). Today, economists are busy calculating the price of rainforests, biodiversity, watersheds, etc., using opinion surveys of "Willingness to Pay" (WTP) to preserve such commons. This forces ordinary citizens to bid for such resources (of no direct benefit to them) against commercial developers who would directly benefit. Such absurd WTP-derived "contingency prices" are hopelessly inaccurate and drastically undervalue common resources. Only calculating the full value of work performed by natural systems and its replacement costs would suffice. *But* these resources are often irreplaceable. So the task is beyond money equiva-

Figure 3
Differing Models of Markets and Commons

Economists	**Futurists/Systems**
Markets Private Sector... • Individual decisions • Competition • Invisible hand • Anti-trust	**Open Systems** • Divisible resources • Win-lose rules • (Adam Smith's rules)
Commons Public Sector... • Property of all • Monopoly under regulation • Consortia	**Closed Systems** • Indivisible resources • Win-win rules • Cooperation • Agreements

Note: One must remember that all such schematizations are, at best, approximations and often culturally arbitrary.

lents and the skills of economists and requires interdisciplinary teams and multiple metrics.[15]

Signs of Change

By January 1999, the "Washington Consensus" view of our global economic future was crumbling. Calls increased for the US to release its "stranglehold over the IMF and the World Bank."[16] The UN Executive Committee on Economic and Social affairs published the report of its task force "Toward a New International Financial Architecture." The report, which was delivered to the G8 in June 1999, Summit states "World events since mid-1997, and in the 1980s and 1990s have made it clear that the current international financial system is unable to safeguard the world economy from financial crises of high intensity and frequency and devastating real effects." The report called for immediate action, with six inter-related reforms:

- improved consistency of macroeconomic policies at the global level
- reform of the IMF aimed at providing adequate international liquidity in times of crisis
- the adoption of codes of conduct, improved information, and financial supervision and regulation at national and international levels
- the preservation of the autonomy of developing and transition economies with regard to capital account issues
- the incorporation of internationally sanctioned standstill provisions into international lending
- a network of regional and sub-regional organizations to support the management of monetary and financial issues

Citizens' movements for re-shaping the global economy were not impressed. Nevertheless the issues are now on the table. Indeed, the report set out that "We must emphasize that any reform of the international financial system ought to be based on a broad discussion, involving all countries, and a clear agenda, including all key issues. The process must ensure that the interests of all groups of developing and transition economies, including poor and small countries, are adequately represented. The United Nations, as a universal and the most democratic international forum, should play an important role in these discussions and in the design of the new system."

After much huffing and puffing, the Group of 7 announced in Bonn, Germany, on February 20, 1999, a new forum "to assess the issues and vulnerabilities affecting the global financial system and to identify and oversee the actions needed to address them." This forum of thirty-five top financial officials of the G-7 countries, the World Bank, the IMF, the Bank for International Settlement (BIS) and various regulatory bodies will meet only twice a year and its only authority will be "peer pressure." Developing countries will be excluded from the forum, while the new BIS-sponsored Financial Stability Institute will add its own ideas. Such insider-driven, top down approaches are unlikely to address any of the fundamental global issues.

The people's agendas go much further—with longer-range reforms at all levels as described in Chapter 3.

Notes

1. H. Henderson, *Paradigms in Progress* (San Francisco: Berrett-Koehler, 1995); *Building a Win-Win World: Life Beyond Global Economic Warfare* (San Francisco: Berrett-Koehler Publishers, 1996, 1997); "Three Hundred Years of Snake Oil," *The Politics of the Solar Age* (Garden City, NY: Anchor Press/Doubleday, 1981).
2. *Human Development Report*, United Nations Development Programme (New York and Oxford: Oxford University Press, 1995).
3. See, for example, H. Henderson, *Harvard Business Review*, July–August, 1973; *Creating Alternative Futures* (New York: Putnam's Sons, 1978, reprint, and West Hartford, Conn.: Kumarian Press, 1996).
4. H. Henderson, *Politics of the Solar Age*.
5. H. Daly and J. Cobb, *Toward the Common Good* (Boston: Beacon Press, 1989).
6. See the US Government's "New Methodology for Calculating Gross Domestic Product," Patrice Flynn, Ph.D., Flynn Research, Harper's Ferry, W.Va., fax: 304-535-9997.
7. H. Henderson, *Paradigms in Progress*, pp. 261–72.
8. M. Reder, *Economics: The Culture of a Controversial Science* (Chicago: University of Chicago Press, 1999).
9. H. Henderson, *Building a Win-Win World*, introduction and ch. 1.
10. Y. Tandon, *Globalization and Africa's Options* (International South Group Network, 1999).
11. "Shifting Fortunes," United for A Fair Economy, Boston, 1999, with forewords by Lester Thurow and Juliet Schor.
12. See, for example, J. Epstein and R. Axtell, *Growing Artificial Societies* (Washington, DC: Brookings Institution Press, 1996), the 2050 Project of Brookings Institute, The Santa Fe Institute, and the World Resources Institute; and R. Pryor et al., "Aspen Model," Sandia National Labs, New Mexico. Also see, P. Ormerod, *Butterfly Economics* (London: Faber & Faber, 1998), which takes economic models as far as they can go.
13. The United Nations University pioneered such work. For example, the Proceedings of its 1984 Symposium in Montpelier, France, *The Science and Praxis of Complexity* (Tokyo: United Nations University, 1984).
14. "Debating the New Economy: Critics Find New Holes in the Data," *Business Week*, July 12, 1999, p. 26.
15. See, for example, NEF's alternative national indicators and the *Calvert-Henderson Quality-of-Life Indicators* soon available at www.calvertgroup.org.
16. *Time*, October 4, 1999, p. 60.

3

BEYOND GLOBALIZATION

The overview of globalization in Chapter 1 highlights the changes in the world economy which have rendered obsolete many current structures, policies, and economic theories. These global changes are accelerating, as a result of ever-closer interlinkages in the new networked information-based world market. Not only are many disciplinary perspectives and metrics required to map these changes, as set out in Chapter 2, but feedback from impacted populations and their advocates is now essential. Kamal Malhotra of Focus on the Global South argues that a "people-centered" reform agenda could be captured in three "subordinations":

- subordination of macro and other economic policy-making goals to human development and social policy goals
- subordination of global level governance mechanisms to those at the local, national, and regional ones, following the principles of subsidiarity
- subordination of the financial "bubble" economy to the real productive economy

Broad public participation by citizens, employees, the poor, and marginalized groups—so greater democracy, equity, and transparency—are requirements for re-shaping the global economy. The successful campaign against the MAI has led to a backlash against more open processes of negotiation. Martin Wolf, writing in the *Financial Times,* argues that "the claims of NGOs to represent civil society as a whole and, as such, to possess legitimacy rivaling—perhaps even exceeding—that of elected governments is outrageous." Such arguments over-generalize, while ignoring the actual functions of pressure groups in modern democracies described by Mancur Olsen in *The Logic of Collective Action* (1965)[1], whether advancing views of business, lobbyists, unions, environmentalists, or groups opposing MAI.

But contrary to many political, expert, and elitist views, such input from citizens is an essential form of expertise. I helped to demonstrate the value of such citizen expertise in spearheading successful public participation programs in science and technology policy-making at the US Office of Technology Assessment from 1974 to 1980.

Much experience with successful civic society inputs has been gained. Civic Society Organizations (CSOs), sometimes still called Non-Government Organizations (NGOs)[2], also went global. They incorporated the expertise of a broad range of new experts under-represented in conventional science. Such citizen groups soon learned that addressing purely local issues on a fragmented basis too often left them blind-sided by powerful global corporations and financial players. They flocked to UN summits on the agendas of "We, the peoples of the Earth": food, habitat, environment, poverty, unemployment, social exclusion, human rights, and ecologically sustainable, equitable human development. CSOs achieved success in campaigns to reform the World Bank, block the MAI and force the issue of debt cancellation onto the international agenda—and many victories in local struggles. Today, voluntary CSOs and civic societies are now recognized as a new "third sector" in all economies. Indeed, in the drive to reshape the global economy and redesign its institutions, civic society is the primary source of social innovation.[3] Thus, with our local experience, common wisdom, and systems approach, we can review the seven system levels from global to local. We can identify many of the new policies, programs, social interventions, and innovations most likely to reshape a global economy aligned with principles of fairness, democracy, human development, and ecological sustainability.

The terms "global," "globalization," and "world" are based in anthropocentric (human-centered) perspectives. They do not include the perspectives of the planet Earth (as seen from space), nor those of all other life forms with which humans share the planetary biosphere. Thus "planetary" is an ecological term embracing natural systems that provide humanity's life support. The relationships between this planetary meta-system and humanity's sub-systems are unsustainable at all levels. Redesigning these human systems, institutions and processes is a pre-requisite for all efforts to rebalance our societies for ecologically sustainable, equitable human development. Population (we now are a six-billion human family) is a key issue, since humans now consume some 40 percent of all the net photosynthesized biomass produced on our planet. Such an *average consumption rate* cannot continue—witness the extinction rates of other species, desertification, climate change and ozone depletion. Yet these averages hide the polarizations of human consumption—with poverty gaps widening as discussed in Chapter 1 between industrial/information OECD countries and people—and those left outside the still-globalizing networks of technology, information, and finance. This is why equitable sharing of the Earth's resources is another key to ecological sustainability.

Therefore, re-shaping the global economy *also* requires including at all levels the missing feedback from nature, planetary and local ecosystems *as well as* the human beings also marginalized by the current runaway forms of globalization. Many "deep ecology" and local self-reliance advocates have called for a rejection and dismantling of large-scale technologies,

TOWARD RESHAPING THE GLOBAL ECONOMY

Level One: *The Global System*, human societies beyond the borders of nations, and their planetary ecosystem effects.

Level Two: *The International System*, including evolving treaties, agreements and unions between nations—beyond the Westphalia system.

Level Three: *The Nation-State*, sovereignty and domestic economic domains.

Level Four: *The Corporate System*, global corporations, charters, and governance.

Level Five: *The Provincial and Local Systems*, small business, local governments, community organizations.

Level Six: *The Civic Society*, voluntary, non-profit groups, the civil sectors from local to global.

Level Seven: *The Family-Individual*, patterns of culture, organization, and behavior

from central electrical generation to TV. Unfortunately, such campaigns, while containing much truth and many workable alternatives, can no longer ignore the realities of today's globe-girdling satellites, jets, TV, and computerized currency-trading, not to mention guided missiles, nuclear weapons and power plants' plutonium wastes. Rejecting globalization based on these powerful technologies is not enough—nor is it feasible. It is hard to imagine how TV, video games, computers, or satellites that relay their content could be repealed. Rather, the colossal task of our generation is to tame these technologies and regulate them—at all levels from global to local—to serve the new goals and purposes of ecologically sustainable, equitable human development. Today, there are aware, motivated, skilled citizens to take on these challenges at all levels and in most countries. The tasks include designing, at all levels, additional dimensions to globalization including more accurate indicators; global monitoring and feedback; higher standards; criteria; better rules; regulations and codes of conduct and principles—embracing human rights, equity, and Earth Ethics.[4] All these must embody better science and information based on new biological knowledge of our relationship to nature. Analysis at every level should be based on a new evolutionary understanding: that nothing less than human survival is at stake. As the late Nobel prize-winner Jonas Salk told me before he died, "We are the first generation in human history in which large numbers of ordinary people are taking personal responsibility for the future of the entire species."

Level One: The Global System
Global Governance

As described in Chapter 1, the accelerating globalization and ensuing deregulation and privatization of finance, markets, electronic commerce have often become destructive flows disordering local societies, cultures, and ecosystems across the planet. Much of the technological prowess on which this globalized economy rests is derived from Cold War military research and development. Huge "defense" budgets (led by the USA) among many industrial and developing countries still rest on the assumption of competing nation-states, the model which first emerged in Europe in 1642 with the Treaty of Westphalia. Each nation guards its sovereignty—making co-operation difficult. In this century, it took two devastating world wars, the failure of the League of Nations and the worldwide depression to create the United Nations in 1945. The Bretton Woods accords in 1944 created the World Bank and the IMF and the General Agreement on Trade and Tariffs (GATT) a limited version of a broader international trade organization, which was opposed by the US. The purpose of these Bretton Woods institutions was to avoid competitive national economic policies and a re-play of the 1930s depression. In addition, currency exchange rates would be fixed—related to a gold standard and overseen by the IMF along with a balance of payments between relative deficits and surpluses in countries' trade and capital accounts. The IMF's member committees (dominated by the US and other rich countries) would govern its policies, lending to countries needing financial assistance under specific terms, interest rates and other conditionalities. The World Bank, still officially called the International Bank for Reconstruction and Development (IBRD) was created largely to reconstruct war-torn Europe. After this bloodiest of centuries with death tolls estimated at one hundred million people worldwide, co-operation is now widely accepted as vital in our now-interdependent world.

The Global Commons

The first task is to address the new threats and dilemmas and to conserve our plantary resources, which are beyond the jurisdictions of nations and current international agreements, treaties, and institutions. Global corporations, banks, speculators, scientific, professional and academic organizations, e-commerce, mass media including the Internet, mercenaries, arms dealers, the Mafia, non-profit humanitarian relief agencies, and voluntary CSOs all roam and rely on this open, largely un-regulated global domain. Often referred to as the global commons, these domains include the oceans, the seabeds, the atmosphere, space, Antarctica, the planet's biodiversity (in forests and natural ecosystems), as well as the Earth's electromagnetic spectrum (the airwaves which carry electronic communications). Legal and constitutional debates abound on extending international law in all these unregulated domains. In *Law in an Emerging Global Village*, (1998), Richard Falk of Princeton University sees "the emergent global civilization as taking shape in the face of a tension between the market-driven forms of globalization and the people-driven modes of resistance as exhibited by trans-national movements to protect the environment, to promote human rights and to challenge the oppression of women and . . . indigenous peoples."[5]

I have argued (1996) that the newest global commons is the Internet and the World Wide Web as well as today's global electronic financial marketplace (since all rely on the Earth's electromagnetic spectrum and the new public domain of cyberspace). All are largely unregulated and with a host of unresolved issues around their use. For example, the Internet's protocol and language codes are still informal and controlled by a handful of early technological innovators and programmers serving as volunteers on ad-hoc standards committees. Worse, while the Internet expands access to information, it is also being rapidly commercialized and is rife with fraud, criminality and pornography. Little legal underpinning exists for this common resource funded by tax dollars and currently overwhelmed by free riders taking advantage of its untaxed status. The muddle in the US over domain names between the profitable Network Solutions, Inc. (NSI) which, amazingly, was *given* this valuable domain name franchise and the new, non-profit ICANN (Internet Corporation for Assigned Names and Numbers) is heading for the courts. In the next few years some kind of "International Internet Standards and Oversight Agency" will be needed to deal with all of these free rider and commons issues and interface with established agencies such as the World Intellectual Property Organization (WIPO) and the International Telecommunications Union (ITU). The European Union has lead the US in systemic thinking about regulating and taxing e-commerce.

Other approaches have been to devise new legal and collective rules toward governing and managing the global commons. A useful overview of the evolution of such governance is by Susan J. Buck at the University of North Carolina, *The Global Commons: An Introduction* (1998). Buck includes a list of six treaties from the 1950s (covering ocean pollution, fishing rights, the continental shelves and Antarctica); five in the 1960s (covering outer space, civil liability, and fauna in Antarctica); fourteen in the 1970s (covering water pollution, also trade in endangered species, wastes and toxics dumping, air pollution, conservation of wild and migratory animals and the Moon); ten in the 1980s (most covering trans-boundary pollution as well as ozone depletion in Montreal, 1987). During the 1990s, the UN Earth Summit in Rio de Janeiro produced the Convention on Biodiversity and the Framework Convention on Climate Change. The Earth Summit's Agenda 21, a comprehensive set of action plans and goals was signed by over 170 governments at Rio. If implemented, Agenda 21 could substantially shift most of the world's countries onto paths toward sustainable development. Yet progress has been sluggish, as the UN Commission on Sustainable Development reported at the "Rio + 5" meeting of the UN General Assembly in New York in 1997.

All this treaty-making has fleshed out global governance well beyond the United Nations Charter signed by fifty-one nations in 1945, which addresses conflicts between states, peace-keeping, human rights, economic and social well-being. The UN's key executive body, the Security Council (peacekeeping) became crippled by the Cold War rivalries of two of its permanent, veto-wielding members, the US and the USSR. The Economic and Social Council (ECOSOC) was supposed to wield similar executive powers, but became weakened by enlargement to fifty-four members in the attempt to overcome wide cultural, social, and economic disagreements over goals and policies. Many now propose a more powerful role for ECOSOC in monitoring the global financial system's social impacts. The Trusteeship Council, the third executive body, needs a new role since few territories remain in "trusteeship" but have become new nations—swelling UN membership today to 187 countries.

Much progress in global governance has been achieved in the fifty-four-year history of the UN. On an annual budget of less than New York City's municipal fire department, the UN has cajoled, networked and convened its member states to agree on a wide range of major global concerns. This has led to many operating agencies, from the ILO, UNICEF, UNDP to UNESCO, FAO, WHO, UNEP, and UNCTAD (respectively concerned with labor, children, education, science and culture, food and agriculture, health, environment, trade and development—for acronyms see Chart I: The United Nations System). The UN is the most inclusive, open and democratic of the global institutions, with its other principal body, the General Assembly of all member-states, as well as its International Court of Justice and Universal Declaration of Human Rights. Partly due to this democratic structure, the rich, powerful countries and financial interests which dominate the IMF and the World Bank Group (including the International Development Association (IDA) and the International Finance Corporation (IFC)) have pulled these Bretton Woods-created agencies away from UN control. Thus today, the World Bank and IMF often act secretively and autonomously. Most CSOs and reports on reform and global governance are concerned about the need for these wayward agencies to return to the UN fold. The successor organization to GATT (a UN body) is now the independent WTO, set up as an intergovernmental body in 1995, but largely dominated by corporate and "free market" agendas. A reformed, democratized WTO is urgently needed. Other bodies operate in crossfires of market and national interests including the ILO's battle with the WTO over labor standards and human rights. UNEP is under fire, over its successful environmental monitoring; WHO now battles private sector interests over rights to healthcare; and UNESCO is attacked over "global heritage sites" it protects, from the Roman baths in Bath, UK to the Grand Canyon in the US.

The Case of Peacekeeping

But the greatest tensions at the UN are of course, over peacekeeping. This is where issues of national sovereignty collide with universal human rights, over national rulers' treatment of their own citizens, whether in

Bosnia and Kosovo or in Chechnya and other breakaway provinces. Big powers, especially the US, have used the UN when its short-term national interests coincide (as in the 1991 Gulf War, which the then US Secretary of State James Baker admitted was as much about oil and jobs as about driving Iraq out of Kuwait); or as a "scapegoat" for US policy failures, as in Somalia. During the US-UN "honeymoon" period after the Gulf War, the UN was seen by US President George Bush as the centerpiece of a "new world order." After Somalia and Bosnia, the atmosphere cooled. The UN was blamed (largely by isolationist US politicians) for the failure of these peace-keeping operations which were mandated by the US-dominated Security Council—but without the necessary follow-up funding. These ill-fated actions together with US withholding of some one billion dollars in back dues precipitated the current financial crisis and US calls for "reform."

The never-completed design for a UN standing force of properly trained peace-keepers illustrates the current set of impasses in the Westphalia system: between the nation-state members of the UN and their sovereignty. While members have systematically limited or stymied collective UN approaches to peace-keeping via the Security Council (which *does* need to be expanded and reformed); Kosovo and the NATO bombing in Yugoslavia have demonstrated the continuing ambivalences over sovereignty. Bypassing international law and the UN (asserting national sovereignty) the US revived NATO with the help of a group of major corporate military contractors and together, with its NATO allies, attacked Yugoslavia on the principle that sovereignty was no longer absolute when major domestic oppression occurred. While this principle is now widely supported, it raised many questions regarding NATO's legitimacy and "mission-creep." Similar shifting of paradigms of sovereignty keep most national leaders silent or in denial about their actual surrenders of sovereignty to global financial markets and the WTO. Perhaps the most important new model is "The Ottawa Process" which produced the Treaty to Ban Landmines, signed by over 160 governments. Pioneered by CSOs and the government of Canada, the campaign over-rode US opposition and earned its co-ordinator, Jody Williams, the Nobel Peace Prize.

Meanwhile, sensible proposals abound to reform the UN Security Council and to admit new members including Japan, Germany, Brazil, India, South Africa, as well as restrict the use of the veto. They languish along with proposals for rapid-deployment humanitarian and standing peace-keeping forces. Meanwhile, many arms budgets resume a spiral upward—led by the US and NATO members. Global arms trafficking is still supported by export policies of the producing countries, mainly the five permanent members of the UN Security Council (the US, UK, Russia, France, and China) as well as Germany. Some workable proposals to address these global issues include a preventive International Deterrent Force (IDF) under Article 43 of the UN Charter, building on similar proposals, which would allow the training of standby peace-keepers as a more credible deterrent before conflicts break out. Such ideas have been advanced by Nobelist John Polanyi (Canada); retired US diplomat Joseph P. Lorenz in *Peace, Power and the United Nations: A Security System for the 21ˢᵗ Century* (1999); the UK's Sir Brian Urquhart in *Toward a More Effective United Nations,* (1992); UN Secretary-General Boutros Boutros Ghali; and the Commission on Global Governance (1996), whose more comprehensive report is mentioned in Chapter 1.

These types of proposals are to backup and bolster preventive diplomacy to head off conflicts—and are seen as funded by reductions in arms budgets. CSOs are leading players, for example, in the global movement; Abolition 2000, with much assistance from the worldwide Buddhist network Soka Gakkai, has gathered over thirteen million signatures to ban nuclear weapons. New global systems of political risk-management are now possible, to deal with today's mostly domestic conflicts and terrorism, centered around strengthening the International Criminal Court. Although the US government foolishly weakened this, a large majority of US citizens (80 percent) approve of a strong Criminal Court. Hopefully, its cases can also be televised before the ultimate court of world opinion. Meanwhile, the International Court of Justice in the Hague, has pioneered the indicting, arresting and prosecution of war criminals.

We can safely reduce the world's military budgets—by employing insurance instead of weapons. For example, the Global Commission to Fund the United Nations has supported the proposed the United Nations Security Insurance Agency (UNSIA), a public-private-civic partnership between the UN Security Council, the insurance industry and the hundreds of civic, humanitarian organizations worldwide which engage in conflict-resolution and peace-building.[6] Any nation wanting to cut its military budget and redeploy its investments into its civilian sectors could apply to UNSIA for a peace-keeping "insurance policy." The insurance industry would supply the political-risk assessors and write the policies. The "premiums" would be pooled to fund both properly trained peace-keepers and a rapid-deployment, on-line network of existing civic, humanitarian organizations "on the ground" to build trust and confidence. The UNSIA proposal is now also backed by several Nobel Prize winners, including Dr Oscar Arias and other leaders, and is taught at the London School of Economics, the Netherlands Institute for Social Studies and other major institutions. The UNSIA concept was debated in the UN Security Council in April, 1996, the first time that body had considered the need to bring civic humanitarian organizations into peace-keeping operations. In May 1996, the Security Council called on the Secretary-General to investigate the feasibility of "a rapid-deployment humanitarian force" and, in October 1996, the Norwegian government pledged one million dollars to this project. The UN now has a new Fund for Prevention to strengthen the Secretary-General's hand for preventive diplomacy.

Certainly the UN's peace-keeping and humanitarianism intervention roles and the International Court of Justice and Criminal Court must be strengthened—together with regional efforts and continued promotion by CSOs of a worldwide culture of peace at all levels. The world can no longer rely on the kind of ad-hoc, "pass-the-hat" funded peace-keeping operations of the late 1990s which brought discredit to the Security Council, member-states and the UN itself. As disarmament treaties and reductions in nuclear and other weapons are pursued, the realization has grown that national sovereignty is limited, and is not always enhanced by military means. The widely accepted concepts of economic, social and environmental security are now calling forth new frameworks viewing such enhanced human well being as "public goods." Producing these "new goods" involves sharing or "pooling" national sovereignty.

Global Public Goods

One of the most important frameworks for dealing with peoples personal and collective security lies in this co-operative production of such "public goods" by all nations. These concepts are spelled out in *Global Public Goods: International Cooperation in the 21ˢᵗ Century* (1999), edited by Inge Kaul, Isabelle Grunberg, and Mark A. Stern (Oxford University Press). Normally, economists think of "public goods" at the municipal and national level as knowledge, health, infrastructure, national parks, defense, and security (e.g., police and justice systems). The ground-breaking concepts in *Global Public Goods* catalogue the broader "menu" of such collectively produced and funded goods and services now necessary for global human security, survival, and development. The definition of global public goods includes those whose benefits reach across borders, generations and population groups, and in addition goes beyond defense, health, and knowledge to include peace, equity, financial stability, and environmental sustainability.

Public goods as we know, are usually underprovided. Since markets often fail, the means to produce them must be organized and created as new "markets," in partnerships with taxpayers, local authorities and national governments. All this requires municipal bonds and public borrowing for public works and investment. These activities also create economic activity, jobs, and deficits—just as does military spending, private sector production, investment, exports, imports, and so forth. The big problem with public goods involves "free riders," the people or companies who end up using the goods without paying their fair share of their costs. Such public goods as parks, education, public services such as health, police, and fire protection which are open to all on a non-excludable basis are termed "positive externalities" by economists. Negative externalities include pollution, species extinction, unsafe products, disease from tobacco use, climate change, and carbon dioxide caused by fossil fuel combustion.

Up to now, all these "negative externalities," which are caused by market failures and less-than-full cost pricing, have been dealt with at global level by the slow, piecemeal passage of regulations, laws and treaties mentioned earlier. Yet with public goods it has been shown in almost every sector, from health care and education to national security and military defense, that prevention costs much less than simply coping with problems after they occur. Diplomacy is much cheaper than war; clean environments and public health measures are cheaper than treating asthma, food poisoning, and epidemics. Standards, rules and regulations can go a long way to steer markets toward democratically set public purposes and goals. But new levels of global cooperation between governments, private sector players and CSOs will be needed to proactively provide the now essential global public goods. Building on the work of creative policy-analysts and economists the contributors to *Global Public Goods* cover their many aspects and sectors requiring such re-organizing of public-private-civic effort. Editor Inge Kaul notes "To turn global public "bads" (pollution, etc.) into global public goods, policy adjustments are needed. Clearly, the dividing line between internal and external affairs has become blurred, international cooperation must form an integral part of national policy-making—and must be a fair proposition for all if it is to be successful."[7] This is also the game-theory approach I took in *Building a Win-Win World* (1996, 1997).

A first step is for all nations to establish externality profiles (i.e., the good and bad "spillovers" they produce beyond their borders). Such national profiles can facilitate realistic bargaining between nations. Similar to ecological footprint[8] analyses, greater transparency on these flows of benefits and adverse impacts between countries can guide all concerned politicians, business people, and CSOs to mutually agreeable policy compacts. Examples include the new joint-implementation agreements such as those emerging out of the climate change conferences in Kyoto (1997) and Buenos Aires (1998). Many tough negotiating sessions are still needed on new approaches to equity between the OECD and developing countries, such as the convergence strategies promoted by The Global Commons Institute in the UK, per capita-based emissions trading and auctioning—(not *giving* such pollution rights to companies); the workings of Clean Development Mechanism; and the shape of the proposed International Bank for Environmental Settlements (a more democratic, transparent form of "green" IMF).[9]

As the UN has convened all the players since Rio in 1992, many are now "speaking the same language." A majority of the world's scientists affirm that human-made climate change is occurring.

A rearguard of fossil-fueled industries and nations must now face the truth. In 1998, violent weather (a well-documented effect of climate change) cost the world's insurance industry a record US$89 billion—more than all weather related catastrophes in all of the 1980s, according to Munich Re, the world's largest insurer. Such negative externalities from fossil-fueled industries, power generation transport and other sectors have already highlighted the absurdities of continuing government subsidies to these industries—including nuclear power—to the tune of US$750 billion to US$1 trillion per year. Just removing these subsidies would amply cover Agenda 21 estimates of US$650 billion to shift to more sustainable forms of production, goods, and services. Similarly, tax profiles of countries could better address the problems of tax-havens, capital flight, and money laundering. The WTO could review national tax policies over the whole range of such unsustainable subsidies, as well as governments "bribing" corporate relocations with tax "holidays." The MAI could address the social responsibilities of investors, not just their rights.

Global Public Goods reports on many other sectors where agreements and progress can be made. At top level, these include broad "externality exchanges" between countries, which could be convened by appropriate UN bodies, from ECOSOC and UNCTAD to UNEP, ILO, WHO, and UNESCO. One example of this is the WHO's work involving pharmaceutical companies in the need to provide millions of doses of simple vaccines. WHO proposed a Millennium Vaccine Fund for such killers as malaria and other tropical diseases and in global epidemiological surveillance. Prevention can save poor countries billions in health costs, lost production, and so forth and, with the right global compacts, can also be profitable for the drug companies. Even former "shock-treatment" Harvard economist Jeffrey Sachs now promotes such programs after seeing the debacles caused by "free market" policies in Russia and the failed IMF prescriptions for the Asian economic crises. Today, Sachs consults for the UNDP and WHO and also uses the global public goods framework to examine international development assistance.[10] He stresses the need for regional approaches to public health, environmental protection, telecommunicating *and* financial market regulations and stabilization. Nobelist economist Amartya Sen treats global justice as a public good; Ismail Serageldin of the World Bank sees the preservation of historic cities as a "cultural public good"; Joseph Stiglitz, chief economist at the World Bank and former US Council of Economic Advisors chairman, admits some of the mistakes of his profession and the World Bank and now promotes global public goods, particularly knowledge. J. Habib Sy and Debora L. Span cover respectively, global communications, the Internet and cyberspace as global public goods, while David Hamburg, Jane E. Holl, and Ruben P. Mendez analyze preventing deadly conflict and peace as global public goods.

Level Two: The International System
Needed: New Trade Rules

One thing has been learned in the past decade's tug-of-war between governments and market players: markets need rules. Contrary to economics textbooks' polarization of markets versus regulations, in reality they are two sides of the same coin. Democracies use two forms of feedback from individuals to decision makers: prices in the market and votes to determine policies. But prices must be correct (including social and environmental costs) and votes must be uncorrupted by money. Even free market ideologues acknowledge that "free" markets rely on government regulations. The "invisible hand" belongs to us, not a deity. Markets require property rights, contracts, national and international law, accounting rules and disclosure, enforcement, police, courts, reliable tax collection (for infrastructure, health, education, and other public services) and civic values. Remove such social institutions and markets descend into chaos, criminality, violence, and the Mafia. Yet laissez-faire beliefs that markets are self-correcting die hard.

The unravelling of rules at national level has been accelerated by international trade agreements administered by the WTO on behalf of its 132 members. The direction of the so-called Millennium Round of trade talks therefore forms a critical turning point on the future of the global economy. The trade negotiators' agendas are as long, and as controversial, as ever. The old chestnuts like agriculture and textiles are automatically itemized along with the "built-in" reviews of key issues like intellectual property rights and technical barriers to trade. But also edging their way up the agendas are issues, which, while talked about ever since GATT was launched half a century ago, have now acquired a new urgency. Included within these is a range of social and environmental issues.

These issues were certainly in the sights of GATT's founders, but were squeezed out during various rounds of negotiations, particularly by the US and by some major developing countries. Consequently, the GATT focused more narrowly on tariffs and barriers to trade at the border and consideration of these other issues was turned over to UN bodies such as the ILO, UNEP, and UNCTAD.

The re-emergence of these issues relates to the evolution of the international trade regime. The WTO is, in a process begun in the Uruguay Round, gradually shifting from the simpler approach that stopped at national borders towards an interpretation of trade that encompasses domestic regulations. One example was the WTO ruling against the ban by the European Union of beef containing growth hormones.

The dispute settlement mechanism is coming, inevitably, to one controversial decision after another on social and environmental issues from bananas to fur caught in leg-hold traps, genetically engineered maize, or shrimp-turtles. Each decision prompts international soul-searching about the WTO's constitutional restraints and its remit. Since the establishment of the WTO, there has been a groundswell of public concern about the effects of globalization and liberalization on the environment and people, in particular in developing countries.

As Bernard Gray wrote in the *Financial Times*, February 3, 1998: "The new world trade battle will not be over tariffs or other market restrictions. It will be over regulation. . . . As borders come down in the world economy, the repercussions of inadequate or flawed regulations are becoming more immediate and more likely to cross national frontiers."

At the heart of the multilateral trade system is a principle of non-discrimination. One component of this, established from the start, was the equal treatment by governments of products whether they were imported or domestic. This requirement to treat "like products" alike, however, extends to a ban on discriminating between like products on the basis of how they were produced. Yet, discriminating between products on the basis of how they were produced is fundamental to securing social and environmental improvement.

The WTO has sought to roll back social and environmental policies at national level which are seen to distort trade. The opposite approach should be taken—promoting patterns of trade which are not subsidized by exploitation, pollution, and less than full cost pricing. This surely is the meaning of non-discrimination that those who suffer the effects of discrimination would understand.

There is already a body of global standards, such as ILO conventions on employment, human rights treaties and the Montreal Protocol on CFCs, which should form the basis for common standards and protocols for national action.

National labour legislation exists in many countries. Indeed, it is often exactly what is needed, based on international standards, and local and national tradition and values. The problem too often is that this legislation is not enforced, for reasons ranging from a lack of capacity and competency to corruption, whether in the labour inspectorates, or the courts. This is of course a global problem. There are over a million people in Los Angeles estimated to be working in conditions well below legal health and safety standards, but the authorities simply have not the interest or intention to act.

There is also an increasing range of voluntary social and environmental standards—ranging from animal welfare, fair trade, and workers rights to organic agriculture. These too have drawn in governments and are, perversely, in the firing line of the WTO as a barrier to trade. The European Union Eco Label has been challenged and is targeted by the US-based Coalition for Truth in Environmental Marketing Information Inc. This represents corporations with US$900 billion of worldwide sales and opposes national and international eco-label schemes outright.

We cannot expect all companies to adopt such codes without prompting. Companies operating in specialist ethical markets, such as fair trade coffee, have pioneered their development. Yet many companies do not have the same moral compass. Market pressures do not unequivocally support best practice, particularly for those not attempting to become world-class players—otherwise such practices would already be universal.

Quite apart from securing the right of existence in WTO for voluntary social and environmental standards, there is a need to reconceive international trade regulation along lines of true non-discrimination in order to promote social and environmental standards. One step towards this, at national or international level, would be to place an obligation on all major companies selling products internationally to report their compliance or non-compliance with accredited standards. This would be termed a "social and environmental disclosure" requirement.

This would not lay down how companies should discharge their responsibilities or which standards they should undertake—only that they declare the mechanisms by which they monitor their performance. It would therefore build on existing market trends and emerging standards, such as the OECD Guidelines for Multinational Enterprises, and enable recognition for compliance with such standards, while being flexible to the arrival of new and improved standards.

Rethinking the Washington Consensus

Taming the global casino of unregulated financial trading is the most urgent task of national governments. At last, after a decade of financial shocks and debacles, culminating in the Asian meltdown and the Russian default, the "Washington Consensus" policy log-jam is crumbling. Influential US economists, including Jeffrey Sachs, Paul Krugman, Joseph Stiglitz, and others are re-thinking their positions. Their former colleague Lawrence Summers, now US Treasury Secretary, is as dogmatic as ever.

One essential first step is the cancellation of the debt of the most indebted countries, perhaps based on US Chapter 9 Municipal Bankruptcy Law as proposed by the Vienna-based Kreisky Forum,[11] Jubilee 2000 and others including Kunibert Raffer, for an inter-national bankruptcy process. Many CSOs reject the G-7 endorsed Highly Indebted Poor Countries (HIPC) Initiative of the World Bank and the IMF—even as it was expanded and received US support at their October 1999 meeting. HIPC is regarded not only as too slow and too restrictive but based on unacceptable conditionalities, which have consistently worsened the problem—as Joseph Stiglitz now argues. UNCTAD's 1998 *Trade and Development Report*, called for an international standstill and orderly debt workout mechanism, derived from provisions contained in the US Bankruptcy Code. This is now supported by the UN.

Such a mechanism would enable a nation facing a currency attack to impose a unilateral standstill on debt servicing to ward off predatory investors and give it the necessary breathing space to design a debt reorganization plan before a liquidity crisis turns into a solvency crisis. The standstill decision would then be submitted for approval to an independent panel rather than the IMF to avoid a conflict of interest with the Fund's shareholders. Such a mechanism would avoid "inciting a panic" and be similar to provisions in the WTO allowing countries to take emergency measures. The debt standstill would be combined with "debtor-in-possession" financing so the debtor country can replenish its reserves and get working capital. Such funds for emergency operations would be much less than the scale of recent IMF bail-out operations, which UNCTAD argues have usually come only after the collapse of the currency and are designed to meet the demands of creditors and prevent defaults. The IMF's prescriptions which exacerbated Asia's problems led to a rethink: the establishment in May 1999 of high-interest bearing Contingency Credit Lines so that countries with strong economic policies could have a precautionary line of defense against "financial contagion" (i.e., speculators).

After the Asian meltdowns, debates over the need for currency boards, various kinds of capital controls, and taxation of currency trading increased markedly.[12] These debates continued after the Russian default of August 1998 and the near-bankruptcy and bailout of the Long Term Capital Management (LTCM) hedge fund a few weeks later. On October 30, 1998, UK Chancellor of the Exchequer Gordon Brown announced a consensus among G-7 finance ministers and central bank governors on proposals to change the world's "financial architecture."[13] US Federal Reserve Board Chairman Alan Greenspan's speeches to Congress and others explaining the Fed's assistance in the LTCM bailout used similar terminology. Both Greenspan and US Treasury Secretary Robert Rubin have referred to the destabilizing role of technology and interlinked currency markets as requiring this "new international financial architecture."[14] Calls for such concerted policy development also came from Australia; France; Germany; the UK, whose Prime Minister, Tony Blair, proposed a new Bretton Woods conference; Canada, whose Finance Minister, Paul Martin urged a new global supervisor of financial supervisory bodies—an idea now widely endorsed.

Since then, the introduction of the euro on January 2, 1999, has absorbed eleven formerly traded European currencies—taking them off traders' screens. Many in financial circles believe this has added to the pressure on other important currencies remaining, including those of Hong Kong, Canada, and Australia, the Czech koruna and those in Latin America, particularly the Brazilian real, which fell 40 percent after its flotation on January 15, 1999, but then recovered substantially. Argentina reacted by raising the possibility that it would abandon its peso (already under a currency board) and adopt the US dollar.[15] The next "cliff-hanger" may be in Equador. Clearly, the IMF's financial assistance to the Asian economies and Russia—and even its $41 billion standby line of credit to Brazil—proved inadequate. "The Washington Consensus," paradigm, still exhorts countries to put their domestic economic houses in order, get their fundamentals right and get used to floating exchange rates, whatever their social costs. In this still "pre-contagion" view, preventing currency devaluations and speculative attacks are domestic matters for national policy makers. Nations are clearly not helpless, but the new global contagion and volatility can no longer only be addressed by nations acting alone and long-term solutions will only be reached at the global systemic level.

Few current operators in the global financial system have acknowledged that a well-regulated, transparent, well-functioning system of financial markets is also a global public good. By the same token, as economist Charles Wyplosz states "financial instability is an international public bad."[16] This, acknowledges what CSOs have been saying for years: financial instabilities and crises affect millions of innocent people worldwide. Marginal reforms will not be enough.

Reforming Capital Markets

Currency exchange taxes, as proposed James Tobin (1974) and Lawrence Summers (1989)[17] while he was an MIT professor, are promoted by many CSOs on some four hundred websites. Bruno Jetin from the French-based NGO Association for the Taxation of Transactions to Aid Citizens (ATTAC) discussed the prospects and feasibility of a combination of equitable international taxations. Although many arguments against a Tobin-type tax relate to the technical difficulties of implementing it, ATTAC's position is that the primary obstacles are political. By way of comparison,

Jetin said creating a single European currency was technically much more complicated than implementing a Tobin tax, but the political will has been sufficient to make it a reality. He further argued that a Tobin tax would not necessarily have to be adopted by a majority of nations at once. Tobin-type taxes could initially be developed within regional arrangements—not only in the European Union, which is ATTAC's short-term campaigning objective, but others such as the Common Market of the South (MERCOSUR) or the Association of South-East Asian Nations (ASEAN). ATTAC has also suggested that the threat of capital fleeing to offshore centers could be offset by international punitive taxes on capital flows to and from these centers. In order to reduce financial volatility, Jetin emphasized that the Tobin tax would have to be complemented with other measures, such as capital controls, particularly during moments of speculative currency attacks.

Rodney Schmidt, from the North-South Institute in Canada, argues that many Tobin tax objections could be overcome by using the increasingly centralized financial infrastructure developed by central banks for the interbank or wholesale market for foreign exchange, which is designed to reduce and eliminate settlement risk. The technology and institutions now in place to support this make it possible for tax authorities to identify and tax gross foreign exchange payments, whichever financial instrument is used to define the trade, wherever the parties to the trade are located and wherever the ensuing payments are made. Schmidt believes that relatively simple derivative instruments such as forward contracts would be easy to tax. The Canadian Parliament passed a resolution in April 1999 to study the Tobin tax.

In addition to Tobin-type taxes, proposals have been made to levy taxes on transnational corporation sales on a pro-rata basis, such as "the one percent solution" proposed by Mitchell L. Gold of the International Association of Educators for World Peace, Toronto, Canada. International taxation agreements are proposed by many CSOs to create a "level playing field" enabling national governments to impose progressive taxes on corporations and financial conglomerates without facing capital flight. National taxes of some financial transactions are already commonly used in many countries. Central banks would also have to coordinate to implement the proposals for a "public utility" foreign exchange to audit and tax all trades.[18] Making such trades taxable would require harmonizing national collections and agreements to curb trades shifting to tax-havens. My proposal with Alan F. Kay for a Foreign Exchange Transaction Reporting System, discussed later, does not require concerted action by central banks, but can achieve similar goals; allowing taxation of speculators and proper oversight of their currencies just as they oversee their sovereign bonds.[19]

The IMF Articles of Agreement (Article VI, Section 3) currently still allow member countries to "exercise such controls as are necessary to regulate international capital movements." A 1996 World Bank study notes that as recently as the 1970s, few countries, whether industrial or developing, were without restrictions on capital movements. Capital controls have been a pervasive feature of the last few decades. In the years following the Second World War, capital controls for macro-economic reasons were generally imposed on outflows of funds as part of policies dealing with balance of payments difficulties and in order to avoid or reduce devaluations. When freer capital movements were allowed from the 1960s onwards, large capital inflows posed problems for rich countries such as Germany, the Netherlands and Switzerland, which imposed controls such as limits on non-residents' purchase of local debt securities and on bank deposits on non-residents. In spite of this history, capital controls were still opposed by the US and the UK, according to London's *Financial Times*, October 30, 1998. The G-7 merely called on governments to make their currency reserves, fiscal and monetary policies more transparent via an "international code of conduct." This will be a step forward only if their proposals for similar codes of conduct can be imposed on central and private banks, trans-national corporations (TNCs) and international speculators.

Institutional Reform

Back in 1995, at the UN Summit on Social Development at Copenhagen a set of proposals emerged in the report of the Global Commission to Fund the United Nations[20] (which this author co-edited), which called for:

- a very small (0.05 percent or less) fee on all currency trades, collected by national governments as proposed by James Tobin

- a global version of the US Securities and Exchange Commission (SEC) to harmonize regulations of securities and currency exchange markets. Such an international supervisory body would curb today's unregulated global casino of insider trading, fraud, money-laundering and capital flight. Today, speculators' "bear raids" attack perceived weak currencies such as those in 1993 which drove the British pound down and out of the European Monetary Union (EMU).

- the proposal, mentioned earlier, derived from UN economic historian Ruben A. Mendez, that the world's major central banks get together and set up their own "public utility" currency exchange

- a new Bretton Woods conference convened by the United Nations— to include all countries in designing co-operative new rules needed to tame the global casino. Since then, the UN has offered its own initial recommendations mentioned in Chapter 1, underlining the world's need to reform the IMF and other financial institutions. But they will also need to be based on new accounting systems that can better monitor long-term investments, ecological assets, human and social capital and can also properly account for unpaid work in the caring sectors of all economies.

Today, a broad campaign based in London at the United Nations Association (see Chart 2 and Directory) promotes A Charter for Global Democracy, supported by the New Economics Foundation and the Global Commission to Fund the United Nations. Its twelve areas for urgent action are aligned with most of those in this book and with the Canadian ten-point Agenda of the Canadian Council for International Co-operation (see Chart 3 and Directory).

Economist Jeffrey Sachs, director of the Harvard Institute for International Development, proposed that the G-7 (which only represents 14 percent of the world's population) should be expanded to G-16 to include eight democratically governed developing countries including Brazil, India, South Korea, South Africa, Chile, and Costa Rica. Sachs has broken ranks with macroeconomists and their "bag of tricks." He notes "for a decade, we have had a phony Washington Consensus—and almost no real discussions between rich and poor countries on the challenges facing a world of greater income inequity than ever before in history. The G-16 would establish parameters for renewed and honest dialogue." Commenting on the Asian crisis, Sachs adds, "The IMF worked mightily and wrong-headedly to make the world safe for short-term money-managers. The IMF encouraged central banks from Jakarta to Moscow to Brasilia to raise interest rates to stratospheric levels . . . investors do not (thus) gain confidence. The more these countries tried to defend their currencies the more they incited panic."[21] This feedback loop was pointed out earlier in the context of interest rate hikes.[22] Many high-level financial officials are now calling for the IMF's role to be expanded to that of a global lender of last resort. Many CSOs would like to curb its powers and even assess the IMF for reparations for economic and social damage it caused in Asian countries. Many economists have reversed their earlier views and cited the need for some small and emerging countries to use capital controls.[23] Few refer to the G-15, a powerful group of developing countries which has met continuously since the late 1980s, and produced an influential report,[24] calling for greatly expanded South-South cooperation. All these proposals should be widely debated.

Not surprisingly, CSOs, citizens, and advocates for those most affected also organized in response to the Asian meltdown. The Bangkok Conference of Focus on the Global South in March 1999 brought together over three hundred experts, parliamentarians, CSO leaders, and international officials to further shape specific policy recommendations.[25] Included were agreements to:

- halt current efforts in the Fund, as well as other fora, to include capital account liberalization in its Articles of Agreement, which would remove the flexibility needed for national governments to introduce capital controls as preventative measures against speculative attacks

- "uncreep" the mission of the IMF back to its original mandate of

financing short-term balance of payment problems without the right
to impose long-term structural reforms on sovereign nations

- support the creation of democratically managed and socially oriented regional monetary funds

In addition, a "World Financial Authority" (WFA) was proposed. Such
an institution (also democratically established and accountable to the United
Nations) would be given executive powers and mandatory sanctions (comparable to those of the WTO) to regulate and oversee both private financial
conglomerates such as hedge funds and global financial institutions such as
the IMF. Its main objectives and tasks would include:

- ensuring that the operations of global financial markets remain
consistent with and promote growth, redistribution, and employment in the real economy

- minimizing systemic risk arising from the operations of securities
and futures markets (for example, by preventing hedge funds from
using borrowed money for speculative purposes, thus avoiding their
highly risky and potentially destabilizing leveraged operations)

- monitoring and regulating the activities of international banks,
currency traders, and fund managers

- ensuring transparency and accountability on the part of International Financial Institutions (IFIs)

- assisting national governments in improving regulatory and control
functions over their national financial systems (for example, through
imposing capital and/or reserve requirements on all major financial
institutions)

- ensuring that the capital controls implemented in one country are
not subverted by neighboring countries pursuing contrary (for
example, financial liberalization) policies to attract finance capital

- providing a forum in which the rules of international financial
cooperation are developed and implemented

Meanwhile, familiar remedies were applied to stem the crises: raising
interest rates, currency pegs, or bands, and so forth. Few heeded the
"trilemma" encoded in the 1962 model of economists Mundell and Fleming,
which warned that countries wishing to inter-link their economies in world
trade cannot simultaneously achieve stable exchange rates, autonomy of
domestic economic policy, and free global capital flows.[26] Ever since the
collapse of Bretton Woods, nations have wrestled with this "trilemma,"
they can achieve two of these goals, but not all three at once.

Other global proposals include investor/philanthropist George Soros's
concept of an International Credit Insurance Corporation to undergird global markets. Soros's analysis is realistic and many of his initiatives move in

the right direction toward the goal of a "global open society" (where enhanced democratic political processes provide a social balance to market processes). However, such an International Credit Insurance Corporation, without additional restructuring of existing financial architecture, might well exacerbate current moral hazard problems. Indeed, Soros offers many other useful proposals to prevent what he sees as a disintegration of the global capitalist system and the evident inability of the international monetary authorities to hold it together.[27]

Soros targets several kinds of derivatives as needing regulation because they engender "trend-following" or herd-behavior, including delta-hedging, "knock-out" options and suggests that all derivatives should be licensed and registered with the US Securities and Exchange Commission (SEC) as "new issues" of securities. Clearly the failure of many of these hedging strategies lies in their models' assumptions of efficient markets and perfect information—points made in Chapter 2 Other remedies widely discussed include imposing margin requirements and "haircuts" on derivatives and other off-balance sheet transactions, as well as regulating hedge funds, banks' proprietary trading operations, and investment banks' in-house hedge funds equally. Interestingly, Soros does not address the issue of speculative currency—trading directly—although he does not deny that he engaged in it and that it is widespread and a factor in current volatility and contagion. Alan Greenspan opposed regulating hedge funds, but did remind us that this increase in volatility is good news for traders, who thrive thereby. Yet few blame traders who are playing by the rules of the current game and are not empowered to change it.

Soros also favors a special loan guarantee fund of at least $150 billion to enable developing countries with sound economic policies to regain access to international capital markets. This idea was floated by US Treasury Secretary Robert Rubin at the IMF annual meeting in October 1998—but received little support. Soros believes such a loan guarantee fund should be financed with a new issue of Special Drawing Rights (SDRs) which, he points out over European bankers' objections, would not create additional money—but would merely fill a hole created by a default.[28] Since then, UK Chancellor of the Exchequer, Gordon Brown has also urged the IMF to create SDRs by selling some of its gold. Soros further believes that IMF conditionalities should have included debt-to-equity conversions of nonperforming loans and tighter policing of banks' capital adequacy ratios by the Bank for International Settlements (BIS). These BIS rules exempted banks from such 8 percent reserve requirements in the case of loans to Korea because it had joined OECD, whose "rich country" membership enjoyed such "low-risk" exemptions. Since then, the BIS has proposed substituting the 8 percent reserve rule with complicated "risk-formulas" for differing levels of risk—while admitting that current risk-analysis models are error-prone (as mentioned in Chapter 2).

Since the Asian crisis, more attention is now devoted to mitigating this systemic risk. The neoclassical assumptions that markets are self-correcting is now severely strained. Many now admit that free markets, trade and capital flows can indeed swamp many small emerging market economies with devastating effects rapidly felt worldwide. Even the London-based *The Economist*, a bastion of free market orthodoxy, has changed its views. The magazine's editorials often call for interventions in markets; cover such formerly taboo subjects as capital controls, tighter bank regulations, and taxing currency exchange; and even advocate Japanese authorities start printing money.[29]

Economist Walter Russell Mead of the elite US based Council on Foreign Relations, Jeffrey E. Garten of Yale University and others address these new issues by proposing an international central bank (first suggested in 1930 by John Maynard Keynes) which could stabilize foreign exchange markets by maintaining its own currency as an international unit of account. Other ideas include reference baskets of currencies (suggested by former US Treasury Secretary James Baker); a "board of overseers" of international financial markets (suggested by Wall Streeter Henry Kauffman); and variations on all these proposals outlined above, from the Institute for International Economic's founder G. Fred Bergsten, (to revive the Japanese proposal for an Asian Monetary Fund), Barry Eichengreen,[30] Jane D'Arista,[31] and others too numerous to mention. The Washington-based Economic Policy Institute's *Taming the Global Casino* (1999) reviews the debate with a useful summary and "Menu of Policy Options" (see Chart 4). While the group considers a Tobin Tax a good idea, it questions how it should be implemented, as well as how the estimate of US$100 to $200 billion in revenues per year would be allocated.

These new proposals, driven largely by pressure from CSOs, should be rigorously studied and debated. Electronic commerce—which is now further loosening central banks' control over money aggregates—deserves particular attention. After all, the technological infrastructure of today's global economy will not be dismantled—indeed it is becoming more complex, interlinked and faster-operating every day.

Level Three: The Nation-State

The Scope for National Action

There are many policy changes which nations acting alone *can* accomplish. Indeed many strategies put forward by CSO leaders including Professor Walden Bello from the University of the Philippines, a founder of Focus on the Global South, are based at the national level—from redirecting GNP-measured growth to land reform. Examples of such national initiatives include Chile's use of taxes and regulations to slow the flows of short-term capital in and out of the country. These partial capital controls have not impeded—and may have enhanced—Chile's record as Latin America's model of stable economic performance in the past fifteen years. China, with its own brand of socialism and growing use of markets has, so far, avoided the ravages of the Asian meltdown, due largely to the inconvertibility of its currency: the yuan (or renminbe). Paradoxically, while the IMF, US, G-7, and other Washington Consensus finance ministers, central bankers and private financiers have long urged full opening of capital accounts and currency convertibility, they have all praised China's stabilizing role in the Asian crisis. By breaking the conventional economic rules, China's yuan and the Hong Kong dollar have remained stable. China, with 1.2 billion people and a permanent member of the UN Security Council, is a world power, with the ability to make its own rules. Devaluation of the yuan would have set off another devastating round of competitive currency de-valuations.

Malaysia's decision in 1998 to install capital-controls and limit con-vertibility of its ringitt broke the conventional economic rules—incurring widespread condemnation and warnings of financial excommunication. Malaysia is one of many small countries which are vulnerable to the US$1.5 trillion of unregulated flows of currency trading. Yet Malaysia succeeded in January 1999 in borrowing US$1.35 billion from a consortium of twelve international banks at only three percentage points over LIBOR. In spite of all the dire threats, Malaysia's rebound in 1999, which some attributed to is capital controls,[32] demonstrated that countries do indeed have options as to how and how much to open their economies to the global market. On September 1, 1999, Malaysia's controls were lifted uneventfully.

These developing countries and smaller economies most at risk, have been aligning their defenses and debating their options individually and through their regional associations, including ASEAN, the UN General Assembly and UNCTAD. There is growing agreement over their rights to control the processes of opening their economies, capital-accounts and cur-rency convertibility. These are sovereign decisions and the IMFs high-handed promotion of Washington Consensus based ideologies and conditionalities for opening capital accounts are now widely rejected. Unilateral policies also include tightening oversight and regulation of domestic banking and corporations' borrowing and central bank supervision of currency markets using fully transparent "best practices" trade reporting, such as the FXTRS[SM] computerized financial control system, described on page 44. Such inde-pendent "virtuous circle" regulating is understood better by game theorists than economists. For example, in the US early in this century, the state of Kansas bucked the lawless trend of lax corporate charters. Yet in two years, twenty-four other states followed Kansas' lead with modern, accountable charter laws. Many states will continue setting their own domestic rules and financial institutions' frameworks according to their own cultures and domestic concerns. This is especially so, since the bouncebacks of Korea, Malaysia, Thailand, and the Phillipines which flouted IMF advice and used Keynesian deficit-spending to stimulate their recoveries. Japan is still try-ing to re-structure its economy, with much conventional economic advice about "opening up" which misunderstands Japanese culture and goals of social stability and full employment. National governments have wide lati-tude to act creatively, without waiting for international agreements or bowing to the dictates of currency traders and corporations.

The Shift to Sustainable Development

One of the positive aspects of the globalization of communications is that domestic obligarchies are exposed, along with social exploitation, poverty and human rights abuses. Thus, many countries' domestic politics are slowly becoming more open and democratic. For example, after Mexico's 1994 meltdown and the US-IMF US$50 billion bailout of international investors and Mexican elites, the exposure of the Fobaproa bank bailout scandal, as well as the Zapatista movement led to the democratizing of the PRI ruling party and more democratic politics. However, the key vulnerabilities to currency flows and speculative attacks remain in all countries. While pushing for a new international financial architecture, countries can also begin national domestic policy shifts that are also needed including:

- implementing the domestic provisions of Action Plans, including Agenda 21 which they pledged at UN Summits. Since the 1972 first Summit on environment, others followed on food, habitat, urban policies, human rights (including women and children), population, poverty, unemployment, and social exclusion. In many countries, cities and provinces have led the way, with local versions of Agenda 21. The UN at these Summits, together with CSOs and the world's media, forced these agendas of "We the Peoples" of the Earth onto the political calendars of recalcitrant national legislative bodies.

- shifting tax burdens from incomes and employment to taxing overconsumption and waste, depletion of natural resources, planned obsolescence, and pollution.[33] Such tax shifting has been urged by Germany's Wuppertal Institute, NEF and the US-based Redefining Progress. The entrenched industries and their political allies have resisted these "green" or ecological taxes. Reforming taxation on land, to re-capture speculative appreciation, is also crucial (as promoted by followers of Henry George including the CSO International Union for Land Value Taxation www.envirolink.org/orgs/earthrights). These tax shifts are revenue-neutral for national budgets—and many companies now support green taxes (for example, the World Business Council for Sustainable Development and other industry representatives who serve on national commissions on Sustainable Development). Germany's new coalition government has announced that it will begin shifting taxes from payrolls and incomes to natural resource use.

- shifting and removing the subsidies to unsustainable industries, products and services. This is also vital, but will be an arduous task. Longtime beneficiaries of these tax largesses and loopholes will continue to fight for them. The huge payoff to global sustainability, as mentioned in Chapter 1, makes it essential to end these subsidies as well as all other special favors to global corporations and investors such as those in the MAI.

- accelerating the statistical overhauls of GNP/GDP and other obsolete macro-economic indicators to account more fully for national resources, including unpaid productive work, as in Agenda 21. These changes must be accelerated, as mentioned, to properly account for public assets, infrastructure, human and natural resources. Canada began its capital budget in 1999 which will account for an additional C$50 billion of formerly un-recorded public investment. While some MPs warned: "this isn't an extra C$50 billion to go shopping with," financial observers and *The National Post* noted that the C$50 billion "will reconcile the books, which have overstated the government-deficit accumulated year after year since the confederation." Such changes in national accounts have radical implications: for lower deficits, fuller employment and reduced interest payments.[34]

In addition, broader indicators balance such narrow, country competitiveness indicators as those of the World Economic Forum and the "Country Risk Indicators" and capital asset pricing models (CAPMs) used by financial markets. National governments can also support the many private, academic and local efforts to design alternative measures of wealth, human development and quality-of-life.

Stabilizing Currency Markets

Among the most immediate actions central banks can take individually is to offer upgraded currency trading systems, such as the Foreign Exchange Transaction Reporting System (FXTRS[SM]), targeted precisely at making foreign exchange trading more efficient and transparent. Once it is adopted by one or two important central banks in OECD or developing countries, it will probably become a global technological standard as others follow suit. Private market players can adopt interfaces in spite of the very small trading fees—simply because the system provides the information they lack and is more efficient. This can also reduce the money-laundering, tax-evasion and criminality which exist in today's unregulated global casino.[35]

Such systems must handle many currency market functions, and reduce the likelihood, scope, and force of a massive bear raid attack on a weak currency. Such attacks have sometimes played a role in crippling the economy of the target currency. Nevertheless, at times and to some degree they are inevitable. FXTRS[SM] systems will not eliminate them, but greatly reduce their likelihood and their severity.

FX traders, per se, are not the cause of the problem; they do not make the rules. On the contrary, traders provide liquidity, with generally razor thin bid-offer spreads and very low transaction costs, which are essential to the satisfactory operation of the US$1.5 trillion global FX market. This is only possible because trader activities, including speculation, produce a market of such enormous size that it is economically possible for both high liquidity and thin margins to co-exist. Those who trade are compensated for supplying the at-risk capital which makes this possible. Bear raids on weak currencies are examples of herd-behavior and can be viewed as battles. On one side are the central banks, whose task is to help manage their domestic currency and economy. They are the only market players ready, if necessary, to sell low and buy high to protect their national economies. On the other side are all others, individuals, banks and all other financial institutions. This includes not just speculators and hedge funds, but anyone who is ready to jump into the fray at some point in hopes of buying low and selling high.

When an economy is weak, there is no doubt that to some extent its currency price should fall. Yet whether a bear raid succeeds does not primarily depend on how over-valued the currency is, but more on how much capital can be brought into the attack and how much capital is fleeing the country. Even sound currencies can succumb to a large enough raid. A bear raid will succeed because of the size of the traders' at-risk war-chests. Even groups of central banks in consort cannot defend against today's huge leveraged hoards of cash.

The bear raid forces an excessive measure of so-called "market discipline" onto countries—even those whose "fundamentals" are sound. The combination of attackers selling the capital and the flight capital of nationals can push the currency to irrationally depressed price levels. Bear raids were prevalent prior to the US 1929 crash. The collapse of the US market and ensuing depression helped elect Franklin Roosevelt president in 1932. In 1934, investment banker Joseph P. Kennedy, father of the late president, John F. Kennedy, was appointed by Roosevelt to head the newly created SEC, which cleaned up the stock market and made it safer for investors. Based on his intimate knowledge of how the US securities markets worked, Kennedy introduced a number of changes in the transaction process itself. One was the "uptick" rule which prevented a broker from selling "short" if the last sale price of a listed stock was lower than the previous transaction price. This slowed the momentum of bear raids and they largely disappeared.[36] Note that this rule utilized "ticker tape" action. "Tickers" now electronic, are based on transaction reporting, at the heart of FXTRS[SM] systems.

Today, with screen-based technology undreamt of in the 1930s, a much smoother process handles the more active global currency markets. Technological designs in the FXTRS[SM] will enable the recording of purposes of trades and counter-parties and help the relevant standards body to curb bear raids without impairing the functioning of the market in normal times and without depriving or slowing the execution of any transaction desired by willing buyer and seller at a mutually agreeable price. These systems would fulfill some of the needs cited by central bankers and finance minister for "a new global financial architecture." The system can be set up to be acceptable both politically and financially to central banks, financial firms and other users, vendors (Reuters, Bloomberg, etc.), foreign exchange brokers and dealers as well as to national political leaders and the public. The participating central banks can assure that all transactions will be promptly reported to the system on a "ticker tape." Trade reporting itself in existing markets generally helps stabilize the market. When a market lacks information, participants must pay for extra research and are still sometimes scared or too easily vacillate between over-caution and recklessness, characteristics exhibited by the global currency markets and their recent volatility, over-and under-shooting. Trade reporting will help smooth currency markets, but further stabilizing mechanisms are still needed.

The transaction fees of 0.001 percent are assumed on all trades of US$1 million equivalent, amounting to US$10 to the buyer of dollars on a base-line trade (or whatever 0.001 percent equals in a base-line trade for the buyer of another currency). That amount is slight compared to other costs and benefits perceived by both parties to any trade. It is reasonable to assume that a charge this small would not derail any trade, or normally even be noticed. However, the basic fee revenue for the system would then be US$10 million per day or about US$3 billion per year if and when all major currency countries were participating. The fuller description of the financial architecture FXTRS[SM] is available from the authors. Patents for FXTRS[SM] are pending at the US Patent office, which will then be donated/ assigned to the United Nations.

Level Four: The Corporate System
Promoting Corporate Accountability

Corporate charters need redrafting to reflect new realities, where knowledge is recognized as a key factor of production and social/environmental performance are benchmarked and audited. Such reforms are advocated by many CSOs, including NEF, TOES-USA, and reformers David Korten, Ward Morehouse, Richard Grossman, Patricia Kelso, Jeff Gates, Australia's Shann Turnbull, and the UK's Godric Bader—many inspired by E. F. Schumacher. While corporate charters are national in some countries, in the US they are chartered by the states. Most corporations, whether global or national, now are accepting the reality that executives manage on the stakeholder model (optimizing among shareholders, employees, customers, suppliers, communities and the environment). The largest survey ever of global public opinion was conducted in October 1999 by Toronto-based Environics International Ltd for the US-based Conference Board and the UK's Prince of Wales Business Leaders Forum. Interviewing 25,000 average citizens in twenty-three countries, the survey found that two out of three want companies to go beyond their historical role of making a profit, paying taxes, employing people and obeying all laws, and to contribute to broader social goals as well.

Legal and financial systems answerable only to shareholders, and "maximizing" shareholders' value must now be re-designed to take the additional stakeholders into account. Many European Union countries, including the

Figure 4
Leading Edge Technologies Mimicking Nature

Some examples of existing successful technologies based on Nature's design:
Cameras mimic the eye; *Airplanes* mimic birds; *Radar* and *Antennas* mimic insects.

Interconnectedness Increasing →

Information Technologies:	Nature's Models:
• **Artificial intelligence**... Expert systems, "hypertext," associative learning program	• **Human intelligence, knowledge** ...Human memory, language
• **Biotechnologies**... Genetic engineering, cloning ...Monoclonal antibodies, interferon, insulin	• **DNA, RNA codes, viruses, bacteria** ...Human immune system
...Gene splicing, hybridization, tissue culture	...Plants, wild species
...Luciferase	...Fireflies
...Pheromones, chemical attractants, biological pest control	...Insects, microbes, fungi
...Protein-based catalysts, assemblers, microbes that "eat" oil spills, sulphur, etc.	...Amino acids ...Microbes
• **Moving beyond medicine that augments the body's defenses and healing process to cell repair and life-extension**	• **Human immune system, DNA, genes**
• **Energy technologies**... Ocean thermal, tidal and wave generators	• **Oceans and other global processes**
...Biomass energy conversion	...Natural decay processes, fermentation
...Dams, hydropower	...Gravity
..."Nanotechnology," molecular assemblers	...Viruses
...Synthetic photosynthesis (zinc pophyrin and ruthenium oxide), photovoltaic cells	...Green plants chloroplasts
...Osmosis, membrane technologies	...Living cell membranes
...Solar arrays and sails	...Insect wings
...Fusion reactors	**...The sun**

UK, are leading this shift. The US is still focused on stock markets and portfolios. Asset managers, pension custodians and security analysts feed national obsessions amplified on market news shows, with short-term stock prices, rapid appreciation and shareholder returns. The US drive to shift corporate charters toward stakeholders, as well as longer-term strategies, is taking place among CSOs and in the socially responsible investing sector (US$1.3 trillion and growing rapidly with sixty-three "ethical" mutual funds (unit trusts) and some forty more in registration).[37]

Social, ethical, and environment auditing, pioneered by CSOs including the US-based Council on Economic Priorities and NEF in the UK, has been adopted widely. Major accounting firms have joined the smaller new consultancies in OECD countries in offering these services. Voluntary corporate codes of conduct and their publication, along with industry and trade association, should be encouraged. Largely driven by external pressures from CSOs, consumers concerned investors and employees these "voluntary" initiatives are important in re-directing corporate goals. Furthermore, they facilitate watch-dog groups and can be assessed and audited.

However, fundamental reform involves shifting all products and processes toward ecological sustainability, as advocated by Sweden's Natural Step, and in Denmark's "industrial ecology" model in Kalundborg. The aim is to mimic natural systems; human innovation has always been inspired by nature (see Figure 4, "Leading Edge Technologies Mimicking Nature" and described in *Biomimicry* (1997) by Janine M Benyus).

Corporate Standards

Voluntary corporate participation in standard-setting—usually with relevant trade associations, government bodies and often with consumer groups as well—dates back over a century. Standard-setting is ubiquitous at all levels—for example, Germany's Blue Angel and US Green Seal and the newer "social" seals of approval such as CEP SA8000 labor standard. All are part of the increasing demands for global corporations to reduce emissions and employ fair labor standards and promulgate Codes of Conduct (e.g., the CAUX and CERES and McBride principles). The clash is escalating between individual value changes, and concern with community and quality of life vis-à-vis market-driven globalization of finance and trade. The ISO 14000 and 14001 standards and Environmental Management Systems (EMAS) and eco-labeling range across products from electrical goods to pharmaceuticals. Corporations continue publishing codes of conduct and fostering such global standards and best practices. (See *Business Week* Special Report, Global Standards, October 1995 and October 1996.) The International Organization of Securities Commissions (IOSCO) has taken the lead in bringing a greater transparency and order to global securities, currency, and futures markets. The big accounting firms and hundreds of new companies are increasing environmental and social accounting and auditing of corporate performance. Many institutional investors and portfolio managers have joined with these business leaders and those which have signed on to the CERES (Coalition for Environmentally Responsible Economies) Principles, the Sullivan and McBride Principles, CAUX Principles, and those of the Social Venture Network and the Minnesota Center for Corporate Responsibility. Concerned asset managers benchmark the Domini 400 Social Index, which regularly out-performs the Standard and Poor's 500. Even the venerable Dow Jones & Company offered its own Sustainability Group Index in September 1999.

United Nations Secretary-General Kofi Annan has urged corporate CEOs to raise these standards of good corporate citizenship.[38] Clear United Nations standards for corporate partners will also do much to dispel the growing suspicions among CSOs and smaller companies that the UN seems to favor the World Business Council on Sustainable Development (WBCSD) and global corporate giants of the industrial era. The UNDP's ill-advised Sustainable Development Fund, with seventeen multi-national corporations, each paying a mere US$50,000, includes many members with poor human rights and pollution records. These companies will be allowed to use a UN logo. Even as the giants strive for eco-efficiency, their power over governments allows them to keep their huge, perverse subsidies, which still hamper the shift to sustainability. Meanwhile, the smaller, cleaner, greener businesses that have been pioneering uphill in the face of such subsidies feel shut out of the very game of sustainable development that they and CSOs have worked so hard for decades to create. It took decades of CSO pressure to get the World Bank to "discover" green technologies, renewable energy, micro-enterprises and micro-credit. The WTO is already in a fire-storm of criticism for its high-handed and ignorant rule-making. The UN can do much better. By proactively embracing ethical and socially responsible small and medium-sized businesses (which are now recognized as the real engines of global job creation), the UN can demonstrate its commitment. Millions of such businesses worldwide can benefit from UN partnerships for sustainable development. The UN can, where necessary, assist those which need help in meeting its standards. Some agencies, including UNICEF and the ILO have shown the lead, others, including UNDP are following suit. Only if we can *raise* the ethical floor under the global corporate playing field can we hope to succeed in the long run.

Disclosure

All of these standards-setting mechanisms as well as eco-labels and the newer human rights labels, (not to mention user-fees, taxation, and fines), are important mechanisms for the shift to sustainability. Indeed, it will take an array of such policy mechanisms including social and environmental auditing of corporations, full-cost pricing, life-cycle costing, and integrating social and environmental costs into capital asset pricing models (CAPMs). All these measures can reduce environmental destruction and irrational investments (particularly in the energy sector), and re-direct much of today's entropic world trade. When thermodynamic and economic models of efficiency are aligned, we see that local and provincial efficiencies of scale are correct, as I emphasized in *The Politics of the Solar Age*.[39] A great deal of CSO campaigning at the WTO will be needed to convince WTO rule-makers and governmental representatives of these ecological principles. Nature's rules of production and its food webs are local, not global. But with all WTO policies, equity must be key if we are to address the needs of the two billion people still below the poverty line. The principle of subsidiarity, so widely accepted in the European Unions and the US (as states' rights) could well be used to curb the WTO, the IMF and other undemocratic international agencies.

The Impact of Electronic Commerce

As more businesses move their transactions into cyberspace, what are some key and broader implications? Let us start with electronic commerce. Most companies assume that money-based transactions will monopolize cyberspace through better security, encryption systems, credit card handling, and e-cash systems. However, electronic commerce does not *require*

money-based transactions, but could employ pure information-based transactions (i.e., high-tech barter). The implications of this are clear: money
and information are now equivalent—we are already off the money and
gold standard and on the information standard worldwide. This new understanding is ushering in a widespread de-mystification of money itself, as
well as credit debt and finance. Many researchers linked to the New Economics Foundation cover these issues: James Robertson, Joseph Huber,
myself and others including E. F. Schumacher, Margrit Kennedy, Michael
Linton, Shann Turnbull, Willem Hoogendijk, and Richard Douthwaite (see
Bibliography).

Banks thrive on money-based scarcity and, understandably, are trying
to control cyberspace transactions. Yet today, billions of dollars of services
and goods are bartered each year in the US by corporations and individuals
on PC-based electronic trading networks. Further shifts to "safe haven,"
high-tech barter transactions will help to create full employment and clear
local markets. Local currencies and PC-based trading systems are flourishing in the US, Canada, Europe, Australia, and New Zealand. Today they
are needed in Russia's largely barter economy. On the negative side, tax-
evaders are catered to more easily by tax-havens, deliberately offering
anonymity, dummy corporations, and money-laundering. Internet-based
commerce and trading make all of this easier.[40]

Giant global retailers, services chains, and mall developers increasingly
displace local merchants. These global TNCs still operate as free riders on
tax-supported infrastructures at below-cost energy prices and at the exclusion of many social and environmental costs. This allows them to penetrate
local markets with below true cost prices. Then after locals have been put
out of business, they can raise prices without their competition. Development banks, local credit unions, and micro-credit groups should be favored
over branches of large national and global banks free riding on the unregulated info-structures of financial cyberspace. These banks, tied into the global
casino, accept local deposits and paychecks but these funds tend to be "vacu-
umed out" of the local branch bank each day onto the global electronic
funds transfer systems (EFTS) to be lent out worldwide. At average global
interest rates, local communities and businesses can no longer afford these
interest rates to borrow back their own deposits.

Perhaps the biggest paradigm shift involves these new information-
based electronic markets—an underlying reason for the take-off of
Internet-based stocks and IPOs (Initial Public Offerings of their shares).
For example, the success of e-Bay.com, a San Francisco-based start-up, is
based on LETS barter networks, offering a second-hand auction over the
Internet, except that subscribers negotiate in money terms. The implications for stock exchanges and banks are vast. If money-creation and
management as well as money-based transactions and credit-availability
are not overhauled drastically to serve the new needs of twenty-first-cen-
tury consumers, businesses, employees, and investors, they will simply go
around banks and money-based transacting. They will continue shifting to
pure information-based transactions such as high-tech barter, local scrip

currencies and LETS systems, while big businesses employ payments unions and expand counter trade (estimated as some 25 percent of global trade). Banks are busy buying computer and information technology to re-impose scarcity and money-based transactions—particularly on electronic commerce via e-cash, credit and debit cards, virtual banking, and so forth.

However, the new competition from money-free, information-based, high-tech exchange will not go away. Banks and money-based exchange systems are very useful, but they now have competition for their basic functions of intermediation—for which the Internet is ideally suited. For example, a quarter of trading volume on Wall Street now is electronic and bypasses brokers, while floor-based "open outcry" stock exchanges are being replaced weekly. Seats on the New York stock exchange lost half their value in 1998. CSOs can take advantage of this rapid re-structuring of financial markets as it dooms many old elites and entrenched players. For example, women, traditionally shut out of finances' old boy networks, found their niche in socially responsible "green investing," pioneering this sector as security analysts and asset managers. Amy Domini, who created the Domini Social 400 Index; Tessa Tennant, Head of National Provident's "green" investment research unit; Joan Bavaria, founder of the Coalition for Environmentally Responsible Economies (CERES); Alice Tepper-Marlin, founder of the Council on Economic Priorities; Michaela Walsh, Esther Ocloo and Ela Bhatt (of India's SEWA) who together pioneered Women's World Banking; and Susan Davis of Capital Missions, to name a few.

Level Five: The Provincial and Local Systems

Local, municipal, and provincial governments have much power, augmented by subsidiarity rules in most countries. Many rural areas bypassed by the networks and players in the global fast lane can host radical experiments in sustainability, such as that documented in Gaviotas, Columbia (later caught in the crossfires of Columbia's political turmoil).[41] The city of Curitiba, in the state of Parana, Brazil, has become a worldwide showcase of innovative urban re-design for both equity and sustainability. Dozens of cities, like Bremen, in Germany, have designated themselves as Agenda 21 models, as have many states in the US.

Commissions on Sustainable Development showcase such models, as did the 1996 UN Summit on Cities: Habitat II in Istanbul. Such local governments can direct bond issues to promote sustainable developments, public transit and renewable energy; prevent suburban sprawl; help in-fill old city cores; renovate obsolete waterfronts; and encourage sustainable agriculture and energy-efficiency. The US President's Council on Sustainable Development is chaired by Ray Anderson, CEO of Interface Carpet, Inc, a pioneer in the shift from goods to recycled services now "dematerializing" OECD economics. The Commission's May, 1999 Report has a wealth of good examples of local and private initiatives.[42]

Cities are beginning to tame traffic with road-pricing schemes (as in Singapore and some European cities), traffic-calming pedestrian malls, bicycle lanes, car sharing systems, and free or cheap municipal bike check out stands. Zoning rules allow localities to experiment with recycling, solar-energy, energy-efficient developments, and water conservation; they can even process city sewage and sell it as fertilizer, as the City of Milwaukee has done for decades under the label "Milorganite" (now being licensed elsewhere). The city of Shanghai in China is launching a 16 billion yuan (US $2 billion) city-wide environmental cleanup, financed by municipal bonds, which will also provide jobs as polluting old industries are closed down. Many cities are re-connecting with their adjacent agricultural areas by setting up farmers' markets and facilitating the contracting between their citizens and farmers for fresh speciality crops and organically grown produce.

Community economic development and renewal is fostered by many local governments in partnership with local banks, investors and civic organizations. These alliances often lobby together for national policy adjustments such as the US Community Reinvestment Act, which requires banks to invest in such local housing, small business development and new infrastructure facilities. In the US, the Chicago-based Sovereignty Project, a coalition of such local development advocates, has introduced a bill in the US Congress which would allow the US Treasury to lend directly to cities, interest-free, for democratically approved, public works projects, ecologically sound development, new schools, etc. Rather than floating high-interest bond issues, which burden future generations, such sovereignty debts would be repaid back to the US Treasury directly. This was the practice with Canada's central bank until the 1950s.

As mentioned, all countries have the sovereign power to coin their own currency and make such public works loans directly as opposed to the practice, often caused by political pressures from private banks, of loaning the federal funds directly to private banks who then lend on to consumers at market rates of interest. Currently, this fractional-reserve banking system has become the norm in the US. However, many CSOs are now challenging this practice of bringing most of our money into creation as debt to banks. Many believe that the sovereign power of creating a nation's money should not have been ceded to private banks, who can lend it out at interest while only retaining a fraction (usually 8 percent under BIS current rules) in reserves. Other essential strategies for local control and building thriving, home-grown economies include local credit-unions, micro-credit, small banks devoted to local lending, local business development groups, and networks of local venture funders.

Local barter networks and various forms of local currencies and scrip are also vital. These simple direct trading techniques are as old as human communities and used widely in traditional societies and informal sectors worldwide.[43] Western adaptations include Cincinnati's Time Store, a typical "bring and buy, skills and labor exchange" café operating in the late 1890s and Ralph Borsodi's commodity-backed currency "the constant" which circulated in Exeter, New Hampshire, in the 1970s.[44] Today, we re-learn that anyone short of official national currencies can join or start such barter clubs. NEF, its founders and associates continue to promote local currencies and economies, documented in David Boyle's book *Funny Money*. Local communities can engage in as much barter as necessary, including high-tech exchanges using personal computers, local exchange trading systems (LETS) and the many kinds of local scrip currencies now circulating in towns in the USA, Europe, and other OECD countries.

These tools can complement scarce national currencies where monetary policy is ill conceived or too restrictive so as to help clear local markets, employ local people, and provide them with alternative local, purchasing power. Indeed, such local currencies in every state and most cities in the USA during the Great Depression helped local communities survive, as documented in Mitchell and Shafer, *Depression Scrip of the United States* (1984). Local coalitions can also block global retail chains, which can undercut local merchants. Many communities in the US have successfully pressured local, city and county councils to oppose mega-stores and malls which drain local businesses and often demand tax breaks. Many US localities disallow such giveaways of their local taxes and instead assess impact fees. Real estate developers are required to post bonds, in order to pay their fair share of providing the new roads, sewers, police, fire schools, and social services which the new residents will require. When developers play off one jurisdiction against another (a common ploy-even between countries), local coalitions have often educated or thrown out of office, local council members with campaigns against "sprawl" and such bumper stickers as "Growth Raises Taxes."

Level Six: Civic Society

As mentioned, citizens and their movements—non-profit organizations or CSOs—operating at every level of human societies from global to local, are now recognized as distinct sectors separate from markets and governments. Both these "public" and "private" sectors in our economic and political texts must now move over, as the third civic sector takes its rightful place in human affairs. University courses now study these civic sectors; politicians court them; both governments and corporations have learned to respect them. Even the World Bank, in an unpublished study, *Beyond the Washington Consensus: Institutions Matter* (1998) at last allowed that "human capital," civil organizations, social structures, families culture and values must be studied and accounted in economic development.

Civic society is the seat of social innovations covering the Sarvodya Shramadana movement in over eight thousand villages in Sri Lanka; Malaysia's Consumers Association of Penang and Third World Network; the twenty thousand members of Senegal's Committee to Fight for the End of Hunger; PAMALAKAYA, a Philippines group of fifty thousand fishers preserving local fisheries; and DECA Equipo Pueblo, Independencia, Mexico, and its Newsletter, *The Other Side of Mexico*. In the US, the non-profit sector represents 7 percent of the GDP. Big environmental groups are big business, such as the Environmental Defense Fund (with a 1996

Figure 5
The New "Attention Economy"

• As Information-Based Economies Shift to Services
• Time and Attention Become as Valuable as Money

NEW TRADE-OFFS
• People seek New Challenges, Experiences, Personal Growth, and Quality of Life
• Many Opt for Less Income and Urban Stress—More Time with Friends and Family, Community-Involvement, Hobbies
• Traditional Material Goods (even Cars, PCs, VCRs) become Commodities
• Services Grow as % of GNP (opera, movie tickets, music, leisure, sports, events, education, crafts, etc.)

---

income of US$22 million); the Natural Resources Defense Council (1996 income: US$27.9 million); and Greenpeace (1996 income: US$22.9 million). Civic movements helped democratize Chile and Argentina, as did Poland's Solidarity Movement and the "Velvet Revolution" in Czechoslovakia. Consumer co-ops, including Japan's Seikatsu and producer co-ops, such as Spain's Mondragon have become models for many others. Other co-ops have become dominant, such as Switzerland's Central Association of Milk Producers and retailers MIGROS and COOP. The UN has long embraced citizens' organizations supporting its Charter and program goals. The United Nations Associations in most countries and many thousands of CSOs are accredited to work with the UN and recognized officially via ECOSOC and the Department of Public Information, Non-Government Liaison Service, UNESCO, UNIFEM (supporting women's rights and advancement), and the UN Volunteers agency.

Citizens and their organizations, as mentioned, have specific expertise and experience now acknowledged to provide vital feedback for all decision-making. This expertise is now often trusted as providing less biased public interest perspectives than much corporate information, which is necessarily self-serving, or even governments and white papers. Thankless efforts by CSOs to independently assess scientific claims and new technologies are often later verified or proved by events and their impacts on society and ecosystems. Since this book is geared to amplify the efforts of citizen movements and CSOs, this section contains contact information on some groups representative of the thousands now working in every country to re-shape the global economy. Other directories and reference sources for CSOs by country include those of Civicus, a non-profit network in many countries, the UN agencies mentioned above and thousands of web-sites which can be accessed using "tree and branching" methods of networking and communicating.

There are few more serious barriers to the growing influence of CSOs in promoting a more peaceful, equitable and ecologically sustainable global economy than today's commercial media monopolies. These giant corporations dominate television, radio, newspapers and wire services. They, along with many other commercial interests, are taking over the Internet. This kind of "commercial censorship" not only impedes people-to-people communications and suppresses vital information. These advertising-driven media empires promote unhealthy products, corporate propaganda and "green-washing"; portray dysfunctional behavior as entertainment; erode self-images; often glorify violence and pornography; and also promote unsustainable, wasteful consumption patterns and consumerism worldwide. Private media corporations accept few explicit social responsibilities and hide behind slogans about "freedom of speech and the press." Many government-operated media are used as mouthpieces to promote official views and policies. Both "manage" news and relay press releases and briefings uncritically—often exacerbating conflicts and sensationalizing war coverage.

At the heart of CSO activities is the promotion of *alternatives*: policies, viewpoints, lifestyles, cultural critiques, and new visions and scenarios of possible and desirable futures. Today, CSOs are media-literate, often sophisticated communication strategists. They understand the politics of images, theatre, art, and music and use these for "culture-jamming," such as the Vancouver-based Adbusters' relentless spoofing of commercials and advertising and their widespread celebrations of "Buy Nothing Days" in which millions now participate.[45]

Other approaches highlight the often unhealthy effects of advertising; the UNDP 1998 *Human Development Report,* focused on consumption, North and South, refers to many CSO activities and groups working on these issues. One proposal now circulating in the US is a "truth in advertising assurance set-aside" (p. 91) which would remove some of the tax deductibility of corporate advertising (across the board for fairness) and place such funds in a special set-aside account to guarantee the truthfulness of ad claims. CSOs who monitor media and commercial advertising could flag violators and apply to the set-aside fund to prepare counter-advertising, in conjunction with independent TV and media producers. When prepared by CSOs (not government agencies) counter-advertising has proved highly effective, such as the US anti-tobacco ads designed by teenage ex-smokers.

CSO-centered and public-access media, especially TV (due to its costs), have been slow to develop. Today alternative magazines, newsletters, radio, low-power, and public access TV are flourishing—along with the growth of the civic society fed by growing mistrust of both governments and corporations. Examples include INTERPRESS SERVICE, a non-profit news agency run by the Society for International Development in Rome, with offices worldwide, and syndicated to hundreds of major newspapers in twenty-seven languages. Young Asia Television (YATV) founded by Norwegian TV anchor Arne Fjortoft distributes grass-roots programming in Asia; Television for the Environment (TVE) based in London has produced and distributed many programs in partnership with CSOs; and US-based Bullfrog Films is a non-profit distributor of thousands of CSO and grassroots people-centered TV programs. Hundreds of independent producers whose films and TV programs cover important public issues and uncover bureaucratic and corporate scandals survive on the fringes of the media monopolies.

We in OECD countries are well into a new era of the "Information Age." We are moving towards the Age of Knowledge, where scarce human time and attention as well as living ecosystems are recognized as more valuable than money. At the same time, we live in "mediocracies" where a few media moguls now control the attention of billions of people—for better or worse—which has changed politics forever. We are already living in the new Attention Economy,[46] (see Figure 5 — The New "Attention Economy") in Attention Deficit societies where each of us is bombarded with information overload from advertisers, media, politicians, teachers, health providers, not to mention junk e-mail. The good news is that this is forcing us to "go inside ourselves" and ask some pretty basic questions: What do I *want* to pay attention to? Who am I and what do I want written on my tombstone? Such basic defensive reactions will define the growing sectors of our Attention Economies and their inexorable shift from material goods (measured by traditional GNP/GDP per capita), to services and more intangible factors in living standards, measured by the new Quality of Life scorecards. As our economies dematerialize, it will be harder for governments to hype wasteful goods-based GDP-growth in the global economy without also measuring toxic wastes, resource depletion, dirtier, shrinking water supplies, polluted air, unsafe streets, drugs, money-laundering, poverty, and global epidemics.

In mature OECD countries, the limiting factor is now *time* rather than *money*. There are only twenty-four hours in each day and already, in the US for example, the average citizen now spends $9\frac{1}{2}$ hours per day (up from $7\frac{1}{2}$ hours in the 1980s) watching TV, movies, and so forth, or online. If GDPs were re-categorized and re-calculated for the US and similar OECD countries, we would find that these information/services sectors already are dominant. For example, mass media and entertainment form a growing percentage of global trade and tourism is the world's largest industry at 10 percent of global GDP. In response, 28 percent of US citizens are "downshifting"—"tuning out" this dominant culture of information overload and costly mass consumption oriented value system.[47] They are choosing more free time and less money income and moving to quieter, less expensive, rural towns where life is slower and communities are still intact. Consumers are seeking their own (not advertisers') definitions of "quality of life." These Attention Economy characteristics include concern for more caring, attention-based health services geared to self-knowledge, prevention, and wellness, as well as cleaner, "greener" products, eco-labeling and the newer "social" seals of approval.

Finally, it is imperative that at least one global TV/Internet network and hopefully more be devoted to exchanging information on the many paths to sustainable development. Today, global, multi-cultural public ac-

cess TV is now a reality (www.wetv.com). Here again, Canada has provided global leadership in launching WETV (the WE stands for "We the
People" and the "Whole Earth"). Growing bandwidth alongside public
demand for more useful content, quality entertainment, education, children's
programming, and community issues means that public access TV is now
viable as never before. Headquartered in Ottawa, WETV, is a public-private-civic network with state-of-the-art multi-media operations now in
thirty-one countries providing programming for human development—allowing self expression from CSOs and the grassroots on global and local
issues.

We are learning that cultural diversity is as important as bio-diversity,
and both are the bedrock wealth of nations. WETV is growing multi-cul-
turally through program-bartering, sharing and partnering with similar
media. Funded by the humanitarian aid programs of seven countries
(Scandinavia, Netherlands, Switzerland, and Austria, led by Canada's IDRC
and CIDA), WETV has obtained rights to all UN television programming
and is contracting with many local public service producers. It is now opening some ownership to private, socially responsible investors and businesses
who will accept WETV's stringent code of conduct and standards for all
private sector partners. Even more innovative is WETV's proposal for equity participation by civic groups and CSOs which provide programming
for WETV distribution. This kind of entitlement to shares in the company
can both provide incentives for CSO shareholders to build up audiences
and earn dividends when WETV is profitable. Finally, it is launching a TV
series "The Ethical Marketplace" which will cover socially responsible businesses and investing, "green" technologies, social accounting and auditing,
corporate codes of conduct, and global ethical standards setting. Such creative hybrids as WETV are typical of Information Age-based companies
and can help make television a positive tool for showcasing local grassroots
solutions and building the global network of healthy, sustainable locally
controlled economies.[48]

Level Seven: Families-Individuals

We humans are one family and are dependent on the evolving life forms
of Gaia (as the Greeks named their Earth Goddess). The Gaia hypothesis
of James Lovelock and Lynn Margulies that the Earth itself is a living or-
ganism, is widely accepted.

Early and Neolithic human societies, as most research on our prehis-
tory shows, worshipped the Earth as our mother. Theories abound as to
how these matrifocal, often gentle societies slowly transformed into the
domination/submission patterns of the competitive, conflict-prone, patri-
archal nation-states of today. War and peace studies, political and diplomatic
experts, politicians, CSOs working on peace, justice, and sustainability—
must face these great questions of human nature, biology, or
upbringing—every day.[49] Is competition, and suspicion of "the other," us-
versus-them thinking innate or learned? Our answers to these basic questions

form the bases to our strategies for self-defense, security, alliances, and dealing with conflicts—whether over resources, ethnicity, religion, race, gender, or differing worldviews.

Many see our planet as a sort of school, where humans can learn the lessons we need to grow in knowledge, understanding, even wisdom. We know human societies grow—there are now six billion of us—but how can they best continue the fifteen-billion year living evolutionary experiment here on Earth? We are now, whether or not we admit it or like it, a global species. But we are not yet assured of a sustainable future. Or any future, if we cannot control the technological forces we have collectively unleashed— nuclear energy, chemical, and biological weapons. We must abolish these new means of destruction, and turn technology to positive good. Satellites, mass media, global cyberspace and our new knowledge of biology and ecology may yet be re-designed and re-focused to serve our common future.

One thing we do know: human societies are experiencing accelerating re-structuring and global change. We humans are approaching our graduating exams on Earth. If we cannot learn to co-exist and live with other species within biospheric rules, we will become extinct. Life will go on without us. Unprecedented numbers of us now see that global co-operation and new forms of global governance are essential. Many of us are examining our own lives, families and relationships, re-negotiating them toward more collaborative partnerships. As we learn about our own inner lives and motivations, many explore new and old spiritual traditions and learn inner peace.

Our essential task is learning to live wisely—and within the tolerances of nature. While we empower ourselves and our communities, sharpen our research skills, invent new ways to keep businesses and governments accountable and perfect the machinery of public participation, democracy and self-government —we need to expand our awareness and understanding. How do we overcome once-useful survival tools, such as fear of scarcity, the "other," the unfamiliar, and our own death?

In all, our efforts to help oppose injustice, alleviate poverty, and re-shape the global economy to serve people, higher standards, human development, and Earth ethics, we are learning that all these efforts begin at home—with our selves. Former Russian culture minister and Harvard sociologist Pitirim Sorokin in his last book, *The Ways and Powers of Love* (1953), quoted French paleontologist/theologian Pierre Teilhard de Chardin, "when humans truly discover the power of love, it will prove more important than the harnessing of fire."

Notes

1. M. Olsen, "The Logic of Collective Action" (Cambridge: Harvard University Press, 1965).
2. Redefinition of citizen organizations is now crucial, since the WTO defines IBM, Microsoft, GM, and other global corporations as "NGOs."
3. H. Henderson, "Social Innovation and Citizen Movements," *Futures* 25, 1993.
4. See, for example, the *Earth Charter*, circulated worldwide since the UN Earth Summit in 1992 by the Costa Rica-based Earth Council (www.ecouncil.ac.cr) and many similar initiatives.
5. Richard Falk, *Law in an Emerging Global Village* (Ardsley, NY: Transaction Publishers, 1998).
6. H. Henderson, and A. Kay, "A United Nations Security Insurance Agency," *Futures*, February 1995.
7. Kaul, Grunberg and Stern, eds., *Global Public Goods*. UNDP (New York and Oxford: Oxford University Press, 1999).
8. See, for example, M. Wackernagel and W. Rees, *Our Ecological Footprint* (Gabriola Island, British Columbia: New Society Publishers, 1996).
9. G. Chichilnisky, "Development and Global Finance, The Case for an International Bank for Environmental Settlements," UNDP, 1997.
10. *The Economist*, August 14, 1999, p. 17–20, "Helping the World's Poorest."
11. H. Henderson, *Building a Win-Win World: Life Beyond Global Economic Warfare* (San Francisco: Berrett-Koehler Publishers, 1996), ch. 13.
12. See, for example, H. Henderson, "The Breaking Point," *Australian Financial Review*, p. 1–9, December 4, 1998.
13. BBC Online Network, London, October 30, 1998.
14. US Treasury Press Release, "Declaration of G-7 Finance Ministers and Central Bank Governors," October 30, 1998, and remarks by Alan Greenspan, "The Structure of the International Financial System," annual meeting of the Securities Industry, Boca Raton, Fla., November 5, 1998.
15. *The Economist*, January 23, 1999, p. 69, Argentina.
16. *Global Public Goods*, p. 152.
17. H. Henderson, *Building a Win-Win World*, chs. 12–13 and V. Summers and L. Summers, "When Financial Markets Work Too Well: A Cautious Case for a Financial Transaction Tax," *Journal of Financial Services*, no. 3.
18. R. P. Mendez, "Paying for Peace and Development," *Foreign Policy*, no. 100 (Autumn 1995).
19. H. Henderson, and Alan F. Kay, "A Foreign Exchange Trade Reporting System," *Futures*, October 1999, Elsevier Science, UK.
20. H. Henderson, ed., with H. Cleveland and I. Kaul, "The UN: Policy and Financing Alternatives," *Futures*, March 1995, Elsevier Scientific, UK; US edition (Washington, DC: Global Commission to Fund the UN).
21. J. Sachs, "Global Capitalism: Making It Work," *The Economist*, September 12, 1998.
22. H. Henderson and A. F. Kay, *Futures*, May 1996, Elsevier Scientific, UK.
23. *Business Week*, February 8, 1999, pp.64–77, and *The Economist*, "Global Finance" section, January 30, 1999.
24. South Commission, *The Challenge to the South: An Overview and Summary of the South Communism Report* (Geneva, Switzerland: South Commission, 1990).

25. See "Democratizing Global Finance: Civil Society Perspectives on People-Centered Economics," (July 1999) UN Non-Governmental Liaison Service, NGLS roundup, No. 38, and the conference report at www.focusweb.net.
26. The Robert Mundell and J. Marcus Fleming model (IMF Staff Papers, 1962) essentially showed that governments and central banks overseeing open economies cannot simultaneously maintain the independence of their domestic monetary policies, stable exchange rates, and uncontrolled global capital flows.
27. G. Soros, "The Crisis of Global Capitalism," *Public Affairs* (1998).
28. Soros, "The Crisis of Global Capitalism," p. 177.
29. *The Economist*, October 10, 1998, p. 18.
30. B. Eichengreen, *Toward a New International Financial Architecture* (City?: Institute for International Economics, 1999). A useful overview of most current proposals.
31. J. D'Arista, and T. Schlesinger, "Reforming the Privatized International Monetary System," *FOMC Alert* 2, #7-8 (1998), Financial Markets Center. An indispensable journal on global financial issues. www.fmcenter.org.
32. *The Economist*, August 21, 1999, p. 17.
33. See, for example, H. Henderson, "Introduce Green Taxes," *Christian Science Monitor*, July 6, 1990.
34. *Economic Reform*, August 1999, Toronto, Canada.
35. H. Henderson and A. F. Kay, "A Foreign Exchange Transaction Reporting System," *Futures* 31, October 1999.
36. H. Henderson and A. F. Kay, *Futures*, May 1996.
37. See, for example, NEF reports and H. Henderson, "Transnational Corporation and Global Citizenship," (Geneva: United Nations Research Institute on Social Development, 1996).
38. Press Release, "Secretary-General Proposes Global Compact on Human Rights, Labour, Environment," Speech in Davos, Switzerland, January 31, 1999. SG/SM/6881/Rev. United Nations, New York.
39. H. Henderson, *The Politics of the Solar Age* (Garden City, NY: Anchor Press/Doubleday, 1981).
40. "The Disappearing Taxpayer," *The Economist*, May 31, 1997, p. 15.
41. A. Weisman, *Gaviotas: A Village to Reinvent the* World (White River Junction, Vt.: Chelsea Green Publishing, 1998).
42. Presidents Council on Sustainable Development Report, May, 1999. "Towards a Sustainable America," Washington, DC, www.whitehouse.gov/pcsd.
43. See, for example, J. Gelinas, *Freedom from Debt: The Reappropriation of Development through Financial Self-Reliance* (London: Zed Books, 1998).
44. H. Henderson, *Creating Alternative Futures* (West Hartford, Conn.: Kumarian Press, 1978, 1996). E. F. Schumacher, *Small Is Beautiful* (New York: Harper & Row, 1973).
45. WorldPaper, August 1999 (published in six languages, worldwide), Boston, Mass., www.worldpaper.com.
46. H. Henderson, *Building a Win-Win World*, ch. 5. This term has since been picked up by Arthur Andersen and *Wired*, April, 1998.
47. Merck Foundation, Harwood Group, Silver Spring, Md., 1995.
48. The author serves on WETV's Business Advisory Council and is Chair of the Editorial Board for "The Ethical Marketplace" TV series.
49. See, for example, S. Elworthy, *Power and Sex* (Oxford: The Oxford Research Group, 1996).

LIST OF INTERNATIONAL TREATIES

Note: The treaties in this list are the major treaties referred to in the text. Readers may wish to consult the World Wide Web site maintained by the Consortium Information Network (CIESIN) for International Earth Science for more detailed information about treaty status (sedac.ciesin.org/pidb/pidb-home.html).

1954   International Convention for the Prevention of Pollution of the Sea by Oil (London). In force, July 26, 1958. Amended, 1962, 1969.

1958   Convention on the High Seas (Geneva). In force, September 30, 1962.

1958   Convention on the Continental Shelf (Geneva). In force, June 10, 1964.

1958   Convention on the Territorial Sea and the Contiguous Zone (Territorial Seas Convention) (Geneva). In force, September 10, 1964.

1958   Convention on Fishing and Conservation of the Living Resources of the High Seas (Conservation Convention) (Geneva). In force, March 20, 1966.

1959   Antarctic Treaty (Washington). In force, June 23, 1961.

1964   Agreed Measures for the Conservation of Antarctic Fauna and Flora (Agreed Measures) (Brussels). In force, November 1, 1982.

1967   Treaty on Principles Governing the Activities of States in the Exploration and Use of Outer Space, Including the Moon and Other Celestial Bodies (Outer Space Treaty). In force, October 10, 1967.

1968   Agreement on the Rescue of Astronauts, the Return of Astronauts, and the Return of Objects Launched into Outer Space (Rescue Agreement). In force, December 3, 1968.

1969   International Convention of Civil Liability for Oil Pollution Damage (Brussels). In force, June 19, 1975. 1976 Protocol in force, April 8, 1981.

1969   International Convention Relating to Intervention on the High Seas in Cases of Oil Pollution Casualties (Brussels). In force, May 6,

1975. 1973 Protocol in force, March 30, 1983.

1971   Convention on the Establishment of an International Fund for Compensation for Oil Pollution Damage (Brussels). Amended 1976, not in force. In force, October 16, 1978. 1984 Protocol not in force.

1972   Convention for the Conservation of Antarctic Seals (Seal Convention) (London). In force, March 11, 1978.

1972   Convention for the Prevention of Marine Pollution by Dumping from Ships and Aircraft (Oslo Convention) (Oslo). In force, April 7, 1974. Amended March 2, 1983, in force, September 1, 1989. 1989 Protocol not in force.

1972   Convention on International Liability for Damage Caused by Space Objects (Liability Convention). In force, October 9, 1973.

1972   Convention on the Prevention of Marine Pollution by Dumping of Wastes and Other Matter (London Convention), (London). In force, August 30, 1975. Amended 1978, in force March 11, 1989. Amended 1989, not in force.

1973   International Convention for the Prevention of Pollution from Ships (MARPOL). Amended by Protocol of 1978 before entry into force. In force, October 2, 1983.

1973   Convention on International Trade in Endangered Species of Wild Fauna and Flora (CITES), (Washington). In force, July 1, 1975.

1974   Convention on the Protection of the Marine Environment of the Baltic Sea Area (Helsinki). In force, May 3, 1980.

1974   Convention on Registration of Objects Launched into Outer Space (Registration Convention). In force, September 15, 1976.

1978   Protocol Relating to the Convention for the Prevention of Pollution from Ships (MARPOL). In force, October 2, 1983.

1979   Agreement Governing the Activities of States on the Moon and Other Celestial Bodies (Moon Treaty). In force, July 11, 1984.

1979   Convention on the Conservation of European Wildlife and Natural Habitats (Bern). In force, June 1, 1982.

1989   Convention on Long-Range Transboundary Air Pollution (Geneva Convention) (Geneva). In force, March 16, 1983.

1979   Convention on the Conservation of Migratory Species of Wild Animals (Bonn). In force, November 1, 1983.

1980   Convention on the Conservation of Antarctic Marine Living Resources (CCAMLR, Southern Ocean Convention) (Canberra). In force, April 7, 1982.

1980   Memorandum of Intent Between Canada and the United States Concerning Transboundary Air Pollution.

1980   Protocol for the Protection of the Mediterranean Sea against Pollution from Land-Based Sources (Athens). In force, June 17, 1983.

1982   Memorandum of Understanding on Port State Control (Paris).

1982   United Nations Convention on the Law of the Sea (Law of the Sea Treaty). In force, November 16, 1994.

1985   Protocol (to 1979 Geneva Convention) on the Reduction of Sulphur Emissions or Their Transboundary Fluxes by at Least 30 Percent (Helsinki Protocol). In force, September 2, 1987.

1985   Convention for the Protection of the Ozone Layer (Vienna Convention) (Vienna). In force, September 22, 1988.

1987   Protocol (to 1985 Vienna Convention) on Substances That Deplete the Ozone Layer (Montreal Protocol) (Montreal). In force, January 1, 1989. Amended 1990 (London), in force August 10, 1992. Amended 1992 (Copenhagen), in force, June 14, 1994.

1988   Protocol (to 1979 Geneva Convention) Concerning the Control of Emissions of Nitrogen Oxides or Their Transboundary Fluxes (Sofia Protocol). In force, February 2, 1991.

1988   Convention on the Regulation of Antarctic Mineral Resource Activities (CRAMRA) (Wellington). Not in force.

1991   Protocol (to the Antarctic Treaty) on Environmental Protection (Environmental Protocol) (Madrid). Not in force.

1992   Convention on Biological Diversity (Biodiversity Convention). In force, December 29, 1993.

1992   Framework Convention on Climate Change. In force, March 21, 1994.

1994   Agreement Relating to the Implementation of Part XI of the United Nations Convention on the Law of the Sea of December 10, 1982. In force, November 16, 1994.

1997   Convention on the Prohibition of the Use, Stockpiling, Production and Transfer of Anti-Personnel Mines and On Their Destruction. Concluded, September 18, 1997.

1997   Kyoto Protocol to the United Nations Framework Convention on Climate Change. In force, December 11, 1997.

1998   Tampere Convention on the Provision of Telecommunications Resources for Disaster Mitigation and Relief Operations. In force, June 18, 1998.

1998   Convention on Access to Information, Public Participation in Decision-Making and Access to Justice in Environmental Matters (Aarhus, Denmark). In force, June 25, 1998.

1998   Rome Statute of the International Criminal Court. In force, July 17, 1998.

1998   Rotterdam Convention for Certain Hazardous Chemicals and Pesticides in International Trade. In force, September 10, 1998.

1999   Food Aid Convention (London). Concluded, April 13, 1999.

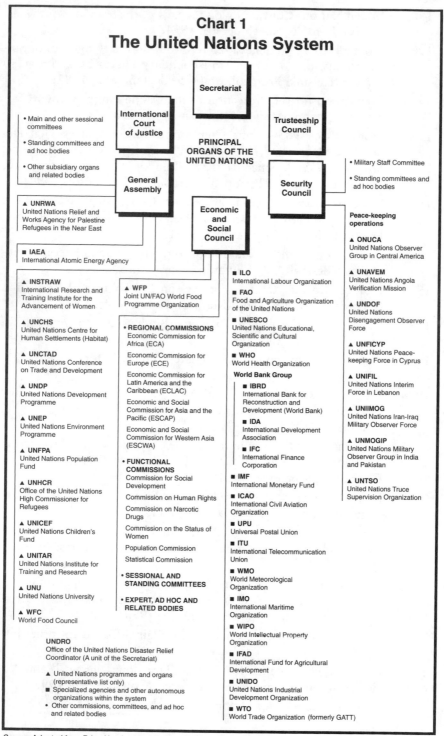

Chart 1
The United Nations System

Secretariat

International Court of Justice

Trusteeship Council

PRINCIPAL ORGANS OF THE UNITED NATIONS

General Assembly

Security Council

Economic and Social Council

- Main and other sessional committees
- Standing committees and ad hoc bodies
- Other subsidiary organs and related bodies

- Military Staff Committee
- Standing committees and ad hoc bodies

▲ UNRWA
United Nations Relief and Works Agency for Palestine Refugees in the Near East

■ IAEA
International Atomic Energy Agency

▲ INSTRAW
International Research and Training Institute for the Advancement of Women

▲ UNCHS
United Nations Centre for Human Settlements (Habitat)

▲ UNCTAD
United Nations Conference on Trade and Development

▲ UNDP
United Nations Development Programme

▲ UNEP
United Nations Environment Programme

▲ UNFPA
United Nations Population Fund

▲ UNHCR
Office of the United Nations High Commissioner for Refugees

▲ UNICEF
United Nations Children's Fund

▲ UNITAR
United Nations Institute for Training and Research

▲ UNU
United Nations University

▲ WFC
World Food Council

UNDRO
Office of the United Nations Disaster Relief Coordinator (A unit of the Secretariat)

▲ United Nations programmes and organs (representative list only)
■ Specialized agencies and other autonomous organizations within the system
• Other commissions, committees, and ad hoc and related bodies

▲ WFP
Joint UN/FAO World Food Programme Organization

• REGIONAL COMMISSIONS
Economic Commission for Africa (ECA)
Economic Commission for Europe (ECE)
Economic Commission for Latin America and the Caribbean (ECLAC)
Economic and Social Commission for Asia and the Pacific (ESCAP)
Economic and Social Commission for Western Asia (ESCWA)

• FUNCTIONAL COMMISSIONS
Commission for Social Development
Commission on Human Rights
Commission on Narcotic Drugs
Commission on the Status of Women
Population Commission
Statistical Commission

• SESSIONAL AND STANDING COMMITTEES

• EXPERT, AD HOC AND RELATED BODIES

■ ILO
International Labour Organization

■ FAO
Food and Agriculture Organization of the United Nations

■ UNESCO
United Nations Educational, Scientific and Cultural Organization

■ WHO
World Health Organization

World Bank Group
■ IBRD
International Bank for Reconstruction and Development (World Bank)
■ IDA
International Development Association
■ IFC
International Finance Corporation

■ IMF
International Monetary Fund

■ ICAO
International Civil Aviation Organization

■ UPU
Universal Postal Union

■ ITU
International Telecommunication Union

■ WMO
World Meteorological Organization

■ IMO
International Maritime Organization

■ WIPO
World Intellectual Property Organization

■ IFAD
International Fund for Agricultural Development

■ UNIDO
United Nations Industrial Development Organization

■ WTO
World Trade Organization (formerly GATT)

Peace-keeping operations

▲ ONUCA
United Nations Observer Group in Central America

▲ UNAVEM
United Nations Angola Verification Mission

▲ UNDOF
United Nations Disengagement Observer Force

▲ UNFICYP
United Nations Peace-keeping Force in Cyprus

▲ UNIFIL
United Nations Interim Force in Lebanon

▲ UNIIMOG
United Nations Iran-Iraq Military Observer Force

▲ UNMOGIP
United Nations Military Observer Group in India and Pakistan

▲ UNTSO
United Nations Truce Supervision Organization

Source: Adapted from Brian Urquhart and Erskine Childers, *A World in Need of Leadership: Tomorrow's United Nations.* Issue of *Development Dialogue 1990*: 1–2 (Uppsala, Sweden: Dag Hammarskjöld Foundation, 1990).

Chart 2

The Charter for Global Democracy:
12 Areas for Urgent Action

Strengthen democratic accountability and participation in international decision-making:

1. Give the UN General Assembly powers to scrutinize the work of UN agencies and other agencies of global governance; create an annual Forum of Civil Society; open international institutions to increased participation by civil society and elected representatives from member countries; bring the WTO into the UN system and strengthen co-operation between all international groupings under the UN system.

2. Create within the UN system an accountable, equitable, and effective mechanism to monitor, supervise, and regulate transnational corporations and financial institutions; and require transnational companies to adhere to an international code of conduct covering agreed principles concerning human rights, the environment, and core labor standards.

3. Give UN institutions an additional and independent source of revenue such as taxation of foreign exchange transactions, aircraft, and shipping fuels, arms sales, and licensing use of the global commons.

Maintain international peace and security:

4. Reform the UN Security Council to open all decision-making to public scrutiny; phase out the single country veto and permanent membership; establish equitable representation from each region of the world; set up a high-level early warning system; and provide effective authority to mediate and intervene in disputes at an early stage, within national boundaries where necessary.

5. Establish a permanent, directly recruited UN Rapid Reaction Force to hold the peace in a crisis, police gross violations of human rights, and support multilateral defence against aggression and genocide.

6. Make the UN register of arms mandatory; ratify and implement the Landmine Ban Treaty; outlaw all weapons of mass destruction; initiate programs to control the arms trade, convert the arms industry to peaceful production and cut military spending worldwide; strengthen accountability to the UN of all international military action; and reduce the size of national armies as part of a multilateral global security system.

Uphold fundamental human rights:

7.   Strengthen world citizenship based on compliance with and respect for the Universal Declaration of Human Rights and all international instruments on Human Rights, including the six core treaties on economic, social, and cultural rights; civil and political rights; racial discrimination; discrimination against women, children's rights, torture, and the conventions on genocide, refugees, and labor standards.

Strengthen justice under international law:

8.   Ratify the Statute of the International Criminal Court; accept compulsory jurisdiction of the International Court of Justice, the International Criminal Court and the UN Human Rights Committee; increase the Courts' powers of enforcement; open the ICJ to individual petition and protect the judicial independence of the ICC.

Promote social progress and better standards of life:

9.   Establish a strong UN institution for Economic and Environmental security to promote international prosperity, protect the global commons, and secure sustainable development.

10.   Establish an International Environmental Court to enforce international treaties on the environment and protect the global commons.

11.   Declare climate change to be an essential global security interest and establish a high-level international urgent action team to assist the UN Conference of the Parties on Climate Change to set a scientifically based global ceiling on greenhouse gas emissions, to allocate national shares of permissible emissions based on convergence to equal per capita rights, and to work with governments, companies, international agencies, and NGOs to cut emissions of greenhouse gases to a sustainable level.

12.   Make poverty reduction a global priority: secure universal access to safe drinking water, health care, housing, education, family planning, gender equality, sustainable development, and economic opportunities, and strengthen the capacity of development agencies to eliminate malnutrition, preventable diseases, and absolute poverty through conservation and equitable sharing of global resources. Cancel the unpayable debts of the poorest nations and institute measures to prevent severe debt burdens from ever building up again.

Chart 3

A Canadian 10-Point Agenda: Meeting the Global Challenge to Eliminate Poverty

The Canadian Council for International Cooperation

1. Promote and accelerate the implementation of commitments for sustainable development made at the 1992 Rio Earth Summit.

2. Make human rights central to the practice of Canadian foreign policy, and in particular seek Canadian and multilateral trade and investment practices that protect internationally agreed labor rights.

3. Build a more equitable global economic order by pursuing trade and investment agreements and regulation of financial flows that contribute to reduced social inequalities and protection of the environment, by canceling unsustainable debt for the highly indebted poorest countries, and by ensuring democratic reform of multilateral trade and financial institutions such as the World Trade Organization, the International Monetary Fund, and the World Bank

4. Ensure NGOs and government fulfill gender equality commitments made at recent global United Nations conferences, with particular emphasis on promoting women's human rights, addressing the feminization of poverty, improving women's participation in decision-making, ensuring women's health, and eradicating violence against women.

5. Fulfill Canada's obligations to improve the lives of children, with measurable progress toward the targets for reducing malnutrition, preventable diseases, and illiteracy set out in the 1990 World Declaration and Plan of Action on the Survival, Protection and Development of Children and on the standards for children's rights in the 1989 UN Convention on the Rights of the Child.

6. Make the world safer for all people by collaborating with all sectors of society to foster locally rooted peace building efforts for war-torn and war-threatened societies and to make common security and peacekeeping core objectives for Canadian defence policy.

7. Promote sustainable food security as a basic human right in Cana-
    dian agricultural and international development policy and work to
    achieve at a minimum the 1996 World Food Summit's seven-point
    Action Plan.

8. Promote corporate social and environmental responsibility and ac-
    countability while seeking a more socially and ecologically balanced
    way of life among Canadians.

9. Reverse the decline in Canadian foreign aid, with a demonstrated
    improvement in poverty eradication through Canadian development
    cooperation over the next five years.

10. Create new opportunities for citizen participation and engagement
    in national and multilateral policy-making, reflecting roles and re-
    sponsibilities for civil societies and political representatives alike,
    promoting more equitable transparent and accountable institutions.

Source: What We Can Do: Global Action against Poverty, 1998. Canadian Council for International Cooperation, Ottawa. www.incommon.web.net.

Chart 4
Menu of Policy Options for Global Financial Reform

Official "new architecture" proposals: making capital markets work better

Increased transparency and disclosure for financial institutions

Improved surveillance by the IMF and other international agencies

Strengthened prudential supervision by domestic regulatory agencies

Better crisis resolution and prevention policies

- reduction of moral hazard in IMF bailouts
- bailing in of creditors, i.e., induce them to keep lending in a crisis
- more orderly debt workouts and bankruptcy procedures
- lending into arrears and in advance of crises

Improved risk management

- private or public credit insurance

Regulating capital flows: cooling down the hot money

Tobin tax on all foreign exchange transactions

- alternative foreign exchange taxes, e.g., Mélitz's 100% short-term foreign exchange profits tax

Capital controls and exchange controls in developing countries

- Chilean-style reserve requirements on short-term capital inflows
- Malaysian-style exchange controls to prevent currency speculation
- stronger restrictions on short-term capital inflows or outflows

Regulation of capital flows in industrialized countries

- prudential regulations on capital outflows, e.g., risk-weighted capital charges on pooled funds
- restrictions on short-term inflows to discourage "safe-haven" investment during financial panics abroad

Creation of more stable channels for development finance

- closed-end mutual fund for emerging market economies

Reforming international institutions

Abolition of the IMF?

- why we need international financial institutions

Proposals for new international institutions

- a world central bank
- an international supervisory institution (board of overseers or world financial authority)
- an international monetary clearinghouse

Fundamental reform of the IMF

- new leadership
- more democratic governance and accountability
- a broader mission: macroeconomic prosperity and social justice
- redesigning rescue packages
  - shifting of adjustment burden more onto creditors via "haircuts," debt relief, etc.
  - less stringent and more appropriate conditionality for debtors, including greater local participation
  - separate short-term goals of crisis remediation from long-term objectives of systemic reforms

Stabilizing exchange rates

Traditional alternatives

- flexible rates
- fixed nominal rates
  - currency boards
  - dollarization
- fixed rates with real targets (adjustable pegs)
- other types of managed rates (e.g., crawling pegs)

Compromise system of managed rates

- target zones with wide, crawling bands
- targets consistent with sustainable current account imbalances
- targets adjusted for inflation and growth differences
- bands that are "hard," with automatic and massive intervention to support them (either by national central banks or an international exchange stabilization fund)

Optimal exchange rate policies varying by type of country:

- target zones for the major currencies (the dollar, euro, and yen, plus other G-7);
- freedom of developing countries to experiment with exchange rate policies that meet their needs

Coordinating macroeconomic policy

Motivations

- to support target zones for exchange rates and discourage speculation
- to give policy-makers more autonomy from financial market pressures Williamson-Miller plan (for major industrialized countries)
- average interest rates targeted on global demand
- interest rate differences between countries targeted on exchange rates
- fiscal policies used for adjusting individual economies to meet national objectives

Modifications and qualifications

- targeting of demand policies on full employment at an acceptable inflation rate
- abandonment of rigid deficit reduction targets to make fiscal policies more flexible
- use of other instruments of credit control to supplement interest rate policy, which would be constricted by the coordination policy
    - e.g., reserve requirements at banks and other financial intermediaries, possibly shifted to assets (loans) rather than liabilities (deposits)

Guiding principles for policy coordination today

- lower average world interest rates to revive growth and prevent deflation
- depreciation of the US dollar in order to reduce the US trade deficit
- pursuit of expansionary demand policies in Europe and Japan to revive their growth and reduce their trade surpluses

Source: Reprinted, by permission, from Robert A. Blecker, *Taming Global Finance: A Better Architecture for Growth and Equity* (Washington, DC: Economic Policy Institute, 1999), 90–91.

SELECTED BIBLIOGRAPHY

Levels One and Two: Global and International

Agenda 21. Volumes I, II, III. E. 92-38352. New York: United Nations, 1993. A simplified version is edited by Daniel Sitars, Boulder, Colo., 1995.

Ayres, Robert U. *Turning Point: The End of the Growth Paradigm*. New York: St. Martins Press, 1998.

Boulding, Elise. *Toward a Global Civic Culture: Education for an Interdependent World*. New York: Teachers College Press, Columbia University, 1988.

Buck, Susan J. *The Global Commons: An Introduction*. Washington, DC: Island Press, 1998.

Carley, Michael and Spapens, Philippe. *Sharing the World: Sustainable Living and Global Equity in the 21ˢᵗ Century*. New York: St. Martins Press, 1998.

Castells, Manuel. *The Information Age: Economy, Society and Culture*. 3 Volumes. Malden, Mass. and Oxford: Blackwell, 1998.

Commission on Global Governance. *Our Global Neighborhood*. New York and Oxford: Oxford University Press, 1995.

Demko, George J. and Wood, William B., eds. *Reordering the World: Geopolitical Perspectives on the 21ˢᵗ Century*. Boulder, Colo.: Westview Press, 1999.

Falk, Richard, *Law in an Emerging Global Village*. Ardsley, New York: Transaction Publishers, 1998.

George, Susan. *The Debt Boomerang* . London: Pluto Press, 1999 reissued.

———. *The Lugano Report: On Preserving Capitalism in the 21ˢᵗ Century*. London: Pluto Press, 1999.

Glenn, Jerome and Theodore, Gordon, eds. *State of the Future*. Washington, DC: The American Council for the United Nations University, 1997, 1998, 1999. Three reports from online conferences of professional futurists from five continents based in academia, business, government, and CSOs. Consensuses were identified in global problems, opportunities, ethical issues, and challenges to global decision-makers at all levels. Website: www.stateofthefuture.org.

Gray, John. *False Dawn: The Delusions of Global Capitalism*. London: Granta Books, 1998.

Greider, William. *One World, Ready or Not: The Manic Logic of Global Capitalism*. New York: Simon and Schuster, 1997.

Hammond, Allen. *Which World?: Scenarios for the 21ˢᵗ Century*. Washington, DC: Island Press, 1998.

Henderson, Hazel. *Paradigms in Progress: Life Beyond Economics*. San Francisco: Berrett-Koehler Publishers, 1995.

————. *Creating Alternative Futures: The End of Economics.* West Hartford, Conn.: Kumarian Press, 1996.

————. *Building a Win-Win World: Life Beyond Global Economic Warfare.* San Francisco: Berrett-Koehler Publishers, 1996, 1997.

Independent Commission on Population and Quality of Life. *Caring for the Future.* New York and Oxford: Oxford University Press, 1996.

Kaul, Grunberg and Stern, eds. *Global Public Goods.* UNDP. New York and Oxford: Oxford University Press, 1999.

Landes, David S. *The Wealth and Poverty of Nations.* New York: W.W. Norton, 1998.

Mayne, Alan J. *From Politics Past to Politics Future: An Integrated Analysis of Current and Emergent Paradigms.* Westport, Conn.: Praeger, 1999.

McMurtry, John. *Unequal Freedoms: The Global Market as an Ethical System.* West Hartford, Conn.: Kumarian Press, 1998.

Peterson, V. Spike and Runya, Anne S. *Global Gender Issues.* Boulder, Colo.: Westview Press, 1993.

Sadruddin Aga Khan, Cameron May, eds. *Policing the Global Economy: Why, How, and for Whom?* (London: Cameron & May, 1998).

Schroyer, Trent, ed. *A World That Works.* New York: Toes Books, Bootstrap Press, 1997.

Singh, Kavaljit. *The Globalisation of Finance.* New York: Zed Books, 1999.

Soros, George. *The Crisis of Global Capitalism: Open Society Endangered.* New York: Public Affairs, Perseus Books Group, 1998.

State of the World annual reports. Published annually. Washington, DC: Worldwatch Institute.

UNDP. *Human Development Report* and all earlier reports since 1990. New York and Oxford: Oxford University Press, 1999.

United Nations Research Institute on Social Development (UNRISD). *States of Disarray.* Geneva: United Nations, 1995. Free, in English, French, and Spanish, Palais de Nations, CH-1211 Geneva-10, Switzerland. Updates available.

Urquhart, Brian and Childers, Erskine. *A World in Need of Leadership: Tomorrow's United Nations.* Issue of *Development Dialogue* 1990: 1-2.

Woodward, David. *Drowning by Numbers.* London: Bretton Woods Project, 1998.

World Commission on Environment and Development. Gro Harlem Brundtland, Chair. *Our Common Future.* New York and Oxford: Oxford University Press, 1987.

Level Three: Nation-States

Ackerman, Bruce, and Alstott, Anne. *The Stakeholder Society.* New Haven, Conn.: Yale University Press, 1999.

Blecker, Robert A. *Taming Global Finance: A Better Architecture for Growth and Equity.* Washington, DC: Economic Policy Institute, 1999.

Frank, Robert H. and Cook, Philip J. *The Winner-Take All-Society: How More and More Americas Compete for Even Fewer and Bigger Prizes, Encouraging Economic Waste, Income Inequality, and an Impoverished Cultural Life.* New York: The Free Press, 1995.

Gelinas, Jacques B. *Freedom from Debt: The Reappropriation of Development Through Financial Self-Reliance.* London: Zed Books, 1998. French edition 1994.

Greider, William. *Fortress America: The American Military and the Consequences of Peace.* New York: Public Affairs, Perseus Books, 1998.

Henderson, Hazel, Flynn, Patrice and Lickerman, Jon, eds. *Calvert-Henderson*

Quality-of-Life Indicators. Washington, DC: The Calvert Group, Inc., 1999.

Ho, Dr. Mae Wan. *Genetic Engineering, Dream or Nightmare?* The Brave New World of Bad Science and Big Business. Bath, UK: Gateway Books, 1998.

Kay, Alan F. *Locating Consensus for Democracy: A Ten-Year Experiment.* St. Augustine, Fla.: American Talk Issues Foundation, 1998.

Krehm, William, ed. *Meltdown: Money, Debt and the Wealth of Nations.* Toronto: COMER Publications, 1999.

Mishel, Lawrence, Bernstein, Jared and Schmitt, John. *The State of Working America.* Washington, DC: Economic Policy Institute, 1998.

Mulgan, Geoff. *Connexity: How to Live in a Connected World.* Boston: Harvard Business School Press, 1997.

Reich, Robert. *The Work of Nations: Preparing Ourselves for the 21ˢᵗ Century.* New York: Knopf, 1991.

Robertson, James. *Transforming Economic Life: A Millennial Challenge.* A Schumacher Briefing. London: Green Books with NEF, 1998.

Rodrick, Dani. *Has Globalization Gone Too Far?* Washington, DC: Institute for Economics, 1997.

———. *The New Global Economy and Developing Countries: Making Openness Work.* Washington, DC: Overseas Development Council, 1999.

Thurow, Lester. *The Future of Capitalism: How Today's Economic Forces Shape Tomorrow's World.* New York: William Morrow, 1996.

Towards a Sustainable America: Advancing Prosperity, Opportunity and a Healthy Environment for the 21ˢᵗ Century. The Presidents Council on Sustainable Development. Ray Anderson and Jonathan Lash, Co-chairs. Washington, DC: The White House, 1999. Surprisingly, this report tackles international financial flows and MAI, as well as leading concepts of industrial ecology, dematerializing, and local initiatives. Website: www.whitehouse.gov.PCSD.

US Office of Technology Assessment. *After the Cold War: Living with Lower Defense Spending.* Washington, DC: US Government Printing Office, 1992.

Wolman, W. and Colamosca, A. *The Judas Economy: The Triumph of Capital and the Betrayal of Work.* New York: Addison-Wesley, 1997.

Level Four: Corporations

Allenby, Braden R. *Industrial Ecology: Policy Framework and Implementation.* Englewood Cliffs, NJ: Prentice Hall, 1999.

Benyus, Janine M. *Biomimicry: Innovation Inspired by Nature.* New York: William Morrow, 1997.

Brill, Hal, Brill, Jack A. and Feigenbaum, Cliff. *Investing With Your Values: Making Money and Making a Difference.* Princeton, NJ: Bloomberg Press, 1999.

Carter, Barry C. *Infinite Wealth: A New World of Collaboration and Abundance in the Knowledge Era.* Boston, London, New Delhi, Johannesburg, and Auckland: Butterworth-Heinemann.

Council on Economic Priorities. *The Corporate Report Card.* New York: Dutton; London, Toronto, and Auckland: Penguin Group, 1998. The Council on Economic Priorities is the first, since 1969, and leading non-profit social, environmental, and ethical auditing group.

Dymski, Gary A. *The Bank Merger Wave.* Armonk, New York: M.E. Sharpe, 1999.

Frankel, Carl. *In Earth's Company: Business, Environment and the Challenge of Sustainability.* Stony Creek, Conn. and Gabriola Island, British Columbia: New Society Publishers, 1998.

Gates, Jeffrey R. *The Ownership Solution: Toward a Shared Capitalism for the*

21st Century. Reading, Mass.: Addison-Wesley, 1998.

Glenn, Jerome C. and Theodore J. Gordon. *1999 State of the Future: Challenges We Face at the Millennium*. Washington, DC: The Millennium Project of the American Council for the United Nations University, 1999.

Gonella, C., Pilling, A., and Zadek, S. *Making Values Count*. London: Association of Chartered Certified Accountants, 1998.

Hawken, Paul. *The Ecology of Commerce*. New York: HarperCollins, 1993.

Hawken, Paul, Amory Lovins, and L. Hunter Lovins. *Natural Capitalism: Creating the Next Industrial Revolution*. Boston: Little, Brown and Company, 1999.

Hopkins, Michael. *The Planetary Bargain: Corporate Social Responsibility Comes of Age*. London: Macmillan Press, 1999.

Kiernan, Matthew J. *Get Innovative or Get Dead: Building Competitive Companies for the 21st Century*. Vancouver: Douglas and McIntyre, 1995.

Knowles, Ross, ed. *Ethical Investment*. Marrickville, NSW, Australia: Choice Books, Australia Consumer's Association, 1997.

Korten, David. *The Post-Corporate World: Life After Capitalism*. San Francisco: Berrett-Koehler and West Hartford, Conn.: Kumarian Press, 1998.

Nattras, Brian and Altomare, Mary. *The Natural Step for Business: Wealth, Ecology and the Evolutionary Corporation*. Gabriola Island, British Columbia: New Society Publishers, 1999.

Savory, Allan with Butterfield, Jody. *Holistic Management: A New Framework for Decision-Making*. Washington, DC: Island Press, 1999.

Weeden, Curt. *Corporate Social Investing: The Breakthrough Strategy for Giving and Getting Corporate Contributions*. San Francisco: Berrett-Koehler Publishers, 1998. A dubious approach which sees co-opting the non-profit sector as vital to corporations.

Zadek, S., Pruzan, P. and Evans, R. *Building Corporate Accountability*. London: Earthscan, 1997.

Levels Five and Six: Civic Society and Localities

Abdullah, Sharif. *Creating a World That Works for All*. San Francisco: Berrett-Koehler Publishers, 1999.

Boyle, David. *Funny Money*. London: HarperCollins, 1999.

Bruyn, Severyn. *A Civil Economy: Transforming the Marketplace in the 21st Century*. Ann Arbor, Mich.: University of Michigan Press, 2000.

Clark, John. *Democratizing Development: The Role of Voluntary Organizations*. West Hartford, Conn.: Kumarian Press, 1990.

Douthwaite, Richard. *Short Circuit*. Devon, UK: Green Books, 1996.

Etzioni, Amitai. *The Moral Dimension: Toward a New Economics*. New York and London: The Free Press, 1988. An influential study of community values and "communitarian" economics.

Fisher, Julie. *Nongovernments: NGOs and the Political Development of the Third World*. West Hartford, Conn.: Kumarian Press, 1997.

Mitchell, Ralph and Shafer, Neil. *Depression Scrip of the United States and Canada*. Iola, Wis.: Krause Publications, 1984.

Sachs, Wolfgang, Loske, Reinhard and Linz, Manfred, et al. *Greening the North: A Post Industrial Blueprint for Ecology and Equity*. London: Zed Books, 1998.

Level Seven: Families-Individuals

Dominguez, Joe and Robin, Vicki. *Your Money or Your Life*. New York and London: Viking, Penguin Group, 1992. The perennial best-seller that spawned many other life-changing self-help books.

Elworthy, Scilla. *Power and Sex*. Oxford: The Oxford Research Group, 1996.

EthicScan Canada. *Shopping with a Conscience*. Toronto: John Wiley and Sons, 1996.

Kamenetsky, Mario. *The Invisible Player: Consciousness as the Soul of Economics, Social and Political Life*. Rochester, Vt.: Park Street Press, 1999. Philosophy from an ex-World Bank Argentine economist.

Kumar, Satish. *Path Without Destination*. Devon, UK: Green Books, 1992, and New York: William Morrow, 1998. Timeless philosophy from one of Britain's outstanding activists and founder of Schumacher College, editor of *Resurgence*.

Jackson, Hildur. *Creating Harmony: Conflict Resolution in the Community*. Holte, Denmark: Gaia Trust, 1999, and East Meon, Hampshire: Permanent Publications, The Sustainability Center, 1999.

Shiva, Vandana. *Staying Alive: Women, Ecology and Development*. London: Zed Books, 1989.

Shopping for a Better World. The Council on Economic Priorities. San Francisco: Sierra Club Books, 1994. US and editions in German and Japanese.

Shuman, Michael M. *Going Local: Creating Self-Reliant Countries in a Global Age*. New York: Free Press, 1998.

PERIODICALS

Adbusters
Quarterly
Media Foundation
1243 7th Avenue West
Vancouver, British Columbia
Canada

Breakthrough News
Bi-monthly
Global Education Associates
475 Riverside Drive, Suite 1848
New York, NY 10115
USA
Telephone: 212-870-3290
Fax: 212-870-2729
Email: globaledu@earthlink.net
Website: www.globaledu.org

The Changemakers
Bi-monthly
Ashoka-Innovators for the Public
1700 N. Moore Street
Suite 1920
Arlington, VA 22209-1903
USA
Telephone: 703-527-8300
Fax: 703-527-8383
Website: www.ashoka.org

Calcutta Office:
188/3/1A Prince Anwar Shah Road
Calcutta 700 045
India
Telephone: 91-33-483-8031
Fax: 91-33-417-2587
Email: chmakers@giasc101.vsnl.net.in

Civicus World
Bi-monthly – Free to members

Civicus
919 18th Street NW, 3rd floor
Washington, DC 20006
USA
Website: www.civicus.org

The Corporate Examiner
Monthly
Interfaith Center on Corporate
Responsibility
475 Riverside Drive, Room 550
New York, NY 10115
USA
(news on Shareholder Activism)
Fax: 212-870-2023

Development
Quarterly
Society for International
Development
207 Via Panisperna
00184 Rome
Italy
Fax: 39-06-4872170
Email: www.safepub.co.ul

Development Alternatives
Publisher and Editor: Ashok Khosla
Monthly
Development Alternatives and TARA
Technologies
(covers innovative, "green"
technologies and action for
rural advancement)
B-32 Tara Crescent
Qutub Institutional Area
New Delhi 110-016
India
Telephone: 91-11-685-1158

Fax: 91-11-686-6031
Email: tara@sdalt.enet.in

Development Dialogue
Quarterly – Free
Dag Hammarskjold Foundation
Orvre Slottsgatan 2
SE-75310 Uppsala
Sweden
Fax: 46-18-12-20-72
Email: secretariat@dhf.uu.se
Website: www.dhf.uu.se

Earth Island Journal
Quarterly
Earth Island Institute
300 Broadway, Suite 28
San Francisco, CA 94133-3312
USA
Fax: 415-788-7324

Economic Reform
Monthly
COMER Publications
245 Carlaw Avenue, Suite 107
Toronto
Ontario M4M 256
Canada
Telephone: 416-466-2642
Fax: 416-466-5827
Email: wkrehm@ibm.net

Finance and the Common Good
Quarterly
(available in English and French)
Observatoire de la Finance
32 Rue de la Athenee
CH-1206 Geneva
Switzerland
Telephone: 41-22-346-3035
Fax: 41-22-789-1460
Email: office@obsfin.ch
Website: www.obsfin.ch

FOMC Alert
Quarterly – Free
Financial Markets Center
PO Box 334
Philomont, VA 20131
USA
Telephone: 540-338-7754
Fax: 540-338-7757

Email: info@fmcenter.org
Website: www.fmcenter.org

Future Survey
Monthly
World Future Society
7910 Woodmont Avenue
Suite 450
Bethesda, MD 20814
USA
Telephone: 301-656-8274
Fax: 301-951-0394
Website: www.wfs.org/fsurv.htm

Go Between
Bi-monthly – Free
UN Non Governmental Liaison
Service
Palais des Nations
CH-1211
Geneve 10
Switzerland
Fax: 41-22-917-0049
Email: nigs@unctad.org or
         nigs@undp.org

New Internationalist
Quarterly
55 Rectory Road
Oxford, OX4 1BW
United Kingdom
Website: www.newint.org/

Multinational Monitor
Monthly except Bi-monthly Jan/Feb
PO Box 19405
Washington, DC 20036
USA
Fax: 202-234-5176
Website: www.essential.org/monitor/
monitor.html

The Other Side of Mexico
Bi-Monthly
DECA Equipo Pueblo
A. C. Francisco Field
Jurado 51, Col. Independencia
Mexico, D.F. 03630
Telephone: 525-539-0015
Fax: 525-672-7453
Email: pueblodip@laneta.apc.org/

Our Planet
Quarterly – Free
UN Environmental Programme
PO Box 30552
Nairobi
Kenya
Telephone: 2542-621-234
Fax: 2542-623-927
Website: www.ourplanet.com

Radio for Peace International
Progressive News Network
Broadcasting Worldwide from Costa
Rica
PO Box 88
Santa Ana 6150
Costa Rica
Debra Latham, General Manager
Frequencies:
        42mm: 6.975 (AM) MHZ
        19mm: 15.050 MHZ
        13mm: 21.460 MHZ
Email: info@rfpi.org
Website: www.rfpi.org

Refugees
Quarterly – Free
(available in English, French, German,
Italian, Japanese, Chinese, Spanish,
Russian, Arabic)
UN High Commission for Refugees
PO Box 2500
1211 Geneva 2
Switzerland
Website: www.unhcr.ch

Resurgence
Bi-monthly
Rocksea Farmhouse
St. Mabyn
Bodmin, Cornwall
PL30 3BR
UK
Telephone: 44-1208-841842
Fax: 44-1208-841842

Tomorrow
Bi-monthly
Tomorrow Publishing AB
Saltmatargatan 8A
SE-1113 59 Stockholm
Sweden

Telephone: 46-8-33-5290
Fax: 46-8-32-9333
Email: info@tomorrowpub.se

Unesco Sources
Monthly – Free
(available in English, French, Chinese,
Spanish and Portugese)
31 Rue Francois Bonvin
75732 Paris Cedex 15
France
Telephone: 33-01-45-68-45-37
Fax: 33-01-45-68-56-54
Website: www.unesco.org/sources

Whole Earth
Quarterly
PO Box 3000
Denville, NJ 07834
USA
Website: www.wholearthmag.com

World Affairs
Quarterly
Publisher: J.C. Kapur
D-322 Defence Colony
New Delhi 110 024
India
Telephone: 91-11-464-2969
Fax: 91-11-462-8994
Email: WORLDAFFAIRS@INDFOS.
WIPR.OBT.EMS.VSNL.NET.IN

European Office:
1 Chemin du Rond Point
1170 Aubonne
Switzerland
Telephone: 41-21-808-5625
Fax: 41-21-808-8134
Email: HARKAPUR@IPROLINK.CH

Worldwatch
Bi-monthly
Worldwatch Institute
PO Box 879
Oxon Hill, MD 20797-5003
USA
Telephone: 800-555-2028
Fax: 301-567-9553
Email: wwpub@worldwatch.org
Website: www.worldwatch.org

DIRECTORY OF ORGANIZATIONS

Accion Ecologica
Alejandro de Valdez N24-33 y Av. La Gasca,
Casillo 17-15-246-C
Quito
Ecuador
Telephone: 593-2-230676
Fax: 593-2-547516
E-mail: mail1.hoy.net@hoy.net

AFL-CIO/Solidarity Center
Lisa A. McGowan, Senior Analyst IFI
Reform
1925 K Street, NW, Suite 300
Washington, DC 20008
USA
Telephone: 202-778-6357
Fax: 202-778-4601
Email: lmcgowan@acils.org

AISEC (Association Internationale des
Etudiants en Science Economique et
Commerce)
40 Rue Washington
Brussels B-1050
Belgium
Telephone: 32-2-646-2420
Fax: 32-2-646-3764
Email: pai@ai.aisec.org
Website: www.aisec.org

Aktie Stroholm
Loek Hilgerson
Oude Gracht
3511 AR Utrecht
Holland
Telephone: 31-30-231-4314
Email: loek@antenna.nl

Angkor Law Group/Cambodian Bar
Association
HEM Hour Naryth, Attorney at Law
No. 45, Preah Suramarit Blvd.
Office Box No. 7

Phnom Penh
Cambodia
Telephone: 15-918-604
            23-360-545
Fax: 855-23-428-227
Email: hhnaryth@forum.org.kh

Association for the Taxation of
Transactions to Aid Citizens (ATTAC)
Pierre Rousset
International Working Group
30, rue Moliere
Montreuil-sous-Bois 93100
France
Telephone: 33-1-42-87-76-87
            33-1-48-70-42-33
Fax: 33-1-48-59-23-28
Email: Pierre.Rousset@ras.eu.org
Website: www.attac.org

Bank Information Center
Lisa Jordan, Executive Director
733 15th Street NW, #1126
Washington, DC 20005
USA
Telephone: 202-624-0621
Telephone: 202-737-7752
Fax: 202-737-1155
Email: ljordan@igc.org
        bicusa@igc.org

Both Ends
Marie-Jose Vervest, Director
Damrak 28-30
1012 L J Amsterdam
The Netherlands
Telephone: 31-20-623-0823
Fax: 31-20-620-8049

Business for Social Responsibility
609 Mission Street, 2nd Floor
San Francisco, CA 94105-3506
USA

Telephone: 415-537-0888
Fax: 415-537-0889
Website: www.bsr.org

Canadian Centre for Policy
Alternatives
Suite 410, 75 Albert Street
Ottawa
Canada
Telephone: 613-563-1341
Fax: 613-233-1458
Email: ccpa@policyalternatives.ca

Center for a New American Dream
6930 Carroll Avenue
Suite 900
Takoma Park
MD 20912
USA
Telephone: 301-891-3683
Fax: 301-891-3684
Email: newdream@newdream.org
Website: www.newdream.org

Centro de Estudios Internacionale
Alejandro Bendano, President
Apartado 1747
Managua
Nicaragua
Telephone: 505-2660500
505-2785413
Fax: 505-2670517
Email: cei@nicarao.org.ni
        ahen@tnx.com.ni

Charter for Global Democracy
United Nations Association Westminster
Branch
Central Hall, Westminster, SW1P 3AS
UK
Titus Alexander, Westminster UNA, 32
Carisbrooke Road, London E17 7EF, UK
Telephone: 44-208-521-6977
Fax: 44-208-521-5788
Email: titus@gci.org.uk

Civicus, World Alliance for Citizen
Participation
919 18th Street NW
3rd Floor
Washington, DC 20006
USA
Telephone: 202-331-8518
Fax: 202-331-8774
Email: info@civicus.org
Website: www.civicus.org
(with member CSOs in 86 countries)

Coalition for Environmental
Responsible Economies (CERES)
Robert Massie, President
11 Arlington Street/6th fl.
Boston, MA 02116-3411
USA
Telephone: 617/247-0700
Fax: 617/267-5400
Website: www.ceres.org

Consumers Association of Penang
Haji S.M. Mohamed Idris JP, President
228 Jalan Macalister
Penang
10400
Malaysia
Telephone: 604-229-3511
Fax: 604-228-5585
Email: mdidris@cap.po.my

Co-op America
Alisa Gravitz, President
1612 K Street, NW, Suite 600
Washington, DC 20006
USA
Telephone: 202-872-5307
Fax: 202-331-8166

Copenhagen Center on Social
Responsibility
Chief Coordinator: Niels Hojensgard
Ministry of Social Affairs
Holmens Kanal 22
DK-1060 Copenhagen K
Denmark
Telephone: 45-33/92-92-45
Fax: 45-33/92-92-95
Website: http://copenhagecentre.sm.dk

DECA Equipo Pueblo
Adriana Garcia Gruz, Director
Francisco Field Jurado 51
Col. Independencia 03630
Mexico
Telephone: 525-539-0015
            525-539-0055
Fax: 525-672-7453
Email: pueblogen@laneta.apc.org

Development Alternatives Group
B-32, TARA Crescent
Qutab Institutional Area
New Delhi
India 10016
Telephone: 91-11-685-1158
Fax: 91-11-686-6031
Email: tara@sdalt.ernet.in
Website: www.ccouncil.ac.cr

Development Resources Centre
Zane Dangor
PO Box 6079
Johannesburg 200
South Africa
Telephone: 27-11-838-7504

Earth Action
Nicholas Dunlop (International
Coordinator)
17 The Green
Wye
Kent TN25 5AJ
UK
Telephone: 44-1233-813-796
Fax: 44-1233-813-795
Email: wye@earthaction.org.uk
Website: www.earthaction.org

Earth Council and Earth Charter
Edificio INS
9th Floor
San Jose
Costa Rica
Telephone: 506-223-3418
Fax: 506-255-2197
Website: www.ecouncil.ac.cr

Ecological Association "GEEA" IASI
Sorin Tecucianu, President
Project Coordinator
C.P. 1634, O P .7
IASI Romania Europe
6600 Romania
Telephone: 40-94-641181
Fax: 40-33-725611
Email: apgro@mail.dntis.ro

Economic Reform Australia
PO Box 505
Modbury
SA 5092
Australia
E-mail: hermann@dove.net.au
Website: http://dove.net.au/hermann/
erahome.htm

Ethical Trade Initiative
Dan Rees, Director
78-79 Long Lane
London EC1A 9EX
UK
Telephone: 44-207-796-0515
Fax: 44-207-796-0616
E-mail: eti@eti.org.uk

First Nations Development Institute
Rebecca Adamson, President

The Stores Building
11917 Main Street
Fredericksburg, VA 22408
USA
Telephone: 540-371-5615
Fax: 540-371-5725
Website: www.firstnations.org

Focus on the Global South
Professor Walden Bello
Nicola Bullard
C/O CURSI Wisit Prachuabmoh Building
Chulalongkorn University
Phyathai Road
Bangkok, Thailand 10330
Telephone: 66-2-218-7363/64/65
Fax: 66-2-255-9976
Email: Focus@ASC9.th.com
Website: www.focusweb.org

Foundation for Science, Technology and
Natural Resource Policy
Vandana Shiva
105 Raipur Road
Dehra Dun
India 248001
Telephone: 91-135-23374

Friends of the Earth, US
Carol Welch, International Policy Analyst
1025 Vermont Avenue, NW
Suite 300
Washington, DC 20005
USA
Telephone: 202-783-7400 (ext 237)
Fax: 202-783-0444
Email: cwelch@foe.org
Website: www.foe.org

Fundacion Ecos
Rosario Bunge, General Coordinator
Agencia 20-Punta del Este
C.E.P. 56098
Uruguay
Telephone: 59842-7-1252/7-2212/7-1532
Fax: 59842-7-1252/7-2212
Email: ecos@adinet.com.uy
Website: www.fundacionecos.org

Green Korea United
Taehwa Lee, Chief Coordinator,
International
1004 Garden Tower 98-78
Wooni-dong
Chongno-ku
Seoul
Korea
Telephone: 82-2-747-8500

Fax: 82-2-766-4180
Email: environ@chollian.net
Website: www.greenkorea.org

Halifax Initiative
Robin Round, Regional Coordinator
#1009-207 West Hastings Street
Vancouver, British Columbia
V6B 1H7
Canada
Telephone: 604-915-9600
Fax: 604-915-9601
Email: rjr@web.net
Website: www.sierraclub.ca/national/

Heinrich – Boell Foundation/Asia Europe
Dialogue
Jost Wagner, Free Co-Worker/Researcher
c/o Wolfgang Kreissi-Dorfler, MdEP
The Greens in the European
Parliament
Bruxelles
LEO 08 G
Belgium
Telephone: 32-2-2845110
Fax: 32-2-2849110
Email: wagn4401@uni-tricr.de
              wkreissi@europar1.eu.int
Website: www.ased.org

Human Rights Forum
Kinhide Mushakoji, President
5-34-14, Yoyogi, Shibuya-ku
Tokyo 1510053
Japan
Telephone: 81-3-3460-5018
Fax: 81-3-3460-5099
Email: QWD00105@niftyserve.or.

ICFTU-APRO
Ching Chabo, Director, ESP Dept.
Trade Union House, 3rd Floor
Shenton Way 068810
Singapore
Telephone: 65-372-1240
Fax: 65-372-1240
Email: ching@icftu-apro.org.sg

Independent Sector
Sandra Trice Gray, Vice President
1200 18th Street NW, Suite 200
Washington, DC 20036
USA
Telephone: 202-467-6100
Fax: 202-467-6101
Website: www.independentsector.org

IDRC/North-South Institute, Canada
Rodney Schmidt
Research Associate and Director
6 T. T Vien Toan, Cong Vi, Ba Dinh
Hanoi
Vietnam
Telephone: 84-4-766-0469
Fax: 84-4-766-0469
Email: veem@hn.vnn.vn

Industrial Shrimp Action Network
Isabel de la Torre, Coordinator
25415 70th Avenue East
Graham, WA 98338
USA
Telephone: 253-846-7455
Fax: 253-847-5977
Email: isatorre@seanet.com

Institute for Agricultural & Trade Policy
2105 1st Avenue South
Minneapolis, MN 55404
USA
Telephone: 612-870-0453
Fax: 612-870-4846
Email: khoff@iatp.org
Website: www.iatp.org

Institute of Comparative Political Studies
Boris Kagarlitsky, Senior Research Fellow
125319 Moscow Krasnoarmeyskaya 29
Flat #43
Moscow 125319
Russia
Telephone: 7-095-1510684
Fax: 7-095-1517918
Email: gbk@glasnet.ru

Institute for Policy Studies
John Cavanaugh, Director
733 15th Street, NW
Washington, DC 20005-2112
USA
Telephone: 202-234-9382
Fax: 202-387-7915

Institute of World Economics and Politics
Yu Yongding, Director
Chinese Academy of Social Sciences
Janguomenne: dajie St., No. 5
Beijing 1000732
China
Telephone: 8610-6612-6105
                  8610-6433-1692
Fax: 8610-6512-6105
          8610-6433-1692
Email: yuyong@public.bta.net.cn
              yuyd@iwep.cass.net.cn

International Council on Social Welfare
Julian Disney, President
24 Edgar Street
Eastwood NSW
2122 Australia
Telephone: 61-2-9804-8824
Fax: 61-2-9804-8823
Email: jdisney@ibm.net

International Forum on
Globalization
1555 Pacific Avenue
San Francisco, CA 94109
USA
Telephone: 415-771-3394
Fax: 415-771-1121
Email: ifg@ifg.org
Website: www.ifg.org

International Institute for
Environment and Development
Nick Robins
3 Endsleigh Street
London WC1H ODD
UK
Telephone: 44-207-388-2117
Fax: 44-207-388-2826
Email: mailbox@iied.org.
Website: www.iied.org

International Monetary Fund (IMF)
Gita Bhatt
Public Affairs Office
700 19th Street, NW
Washington, DC 20431
USA
Telephone: 202-623-7968
Fax: 202-623-6200
Email: gbhatt@imf.org.

International NGO Committee on Human
Rights And Habitat
International Coalition
Miloon Kothari, Joint-Convenor
8 rue Gustave Moynier
Geneve 1202
Switzerland
Telephone: 41-22-7388167
         91-11-91582413 (India)
Email: hic-hrc@iprolink.ch

International Society for Ecology and
Culture
Helena Norberg-Hodge
Apple Barn
Week, Totnes
Devon TQ9 6JP
Telephone: 44-1803-868650

Fax: 44-1803-868651
Email: isecuk@gn.apc.org
Website: www.isec.org.uk

International South Group Network
(ISGN)
Yash Tandon, Director
7 Dougal Avenue
The Grange
Harare
Zimbabwe
Telephone: 263-4-499876
Fax: 263-4-499079
Email: ytandon@harare.iafrica.com
         ytandon@internet.co.zw

Kairos Europe
Anja Osterhaus
Programma Coordinator
Hegenichstrasse 22
Heidelberg
D-69124
Germany
Telephone: 49-6221-712610
Fax: 49-6221-781183
Email: KAIROSHD@aol.com
Website: c.3hu/-bocs/kairos-dev-edu

Korean Confederation of Trade Unions
(KCTU)
Young-Joo Ko, General Secretary
5th Floor, Daeyoung Building
139 Youngdeungpo-2-Ga
Seoul 150 032
Korea
Telephone: 822-635-1133
Fax: 822-635-1134
Email: kctu@kctu.org
Website: www.kctu.org

Labour Education Foundation
Khalid Mehmood, Analyst Political
Economy
Jeddojuhd Center, 40 Abbot Road
Lahore
Pakistan
Telephone: 92-42-6315162
Fax: 92-42-6301685
Email: ipp@ipp.edunet.sdnpk.undp.org
         Edu@found.edunet.sdnpk

Management and Organisation
Development
Joel Rodriguez, Executive Director
29 Magiting Street, Corner Mahiyain Street
Teachers Village
Quezon City
Philippines

Telephone: 632-435-3652
Fax: 632-435-3655
Email: info@mode.org
       joel@mode.org
Website: www.mode.org

Minnesota Center for Corporate
Responsibility
Robert MacGregor, President
1000 La Salle Avenue, Suite 153
Minneapolis, MN 55403-2005
USA
Telephone: 612-962-4120
Fax: 612-962-4125
Email: MCCR-UST@stthomas.edu

Movement for the Defense of
Democratic Rights
S. G. Punchihewa, Executive Secretary
1149, Kotte Road
Rajagiriya
Sri Lanka
Telephone: 01-865655
Fax: 01-873775
Email: mddr@sit.lk

Mozambican Coalition for
Economic Justice
Viriato Tamele, Coordinator
Avenida 24 de Julho 285
3 andar 6, Maputo
Mozambique
Telephone: 258-1-497-273
Fax: 258-1-496-001
Email: virias@hotmail.com

National Assembly of Republic of Korea
Lee Mi Kyung
#105 Member's Office Bldg.
Yoido-dong, Youngdeungpo-ku
Seoul
Korea
Fax: 82-2-788-3105
Email: lmk2014@assembly.go.kr

National Center for Advocacy Studies
John Samuel, Executive Director
2 Santhosh Appartments
Paud Road, Pune
Sheelavihar Colony Maharashtra
411038
India
Telephone: 91-20-346-460
Fax: 91-20-346-460
Email: ncas@wmi.co.in
       ncas@vsnl.com

National Foundation for Women Business
Owners

1100 Wayne Avenue, Suite 830
Silver Spring, MD 20910-5603
USA
Telephone: 301-495-4975
Fax: 301-495-4979
Website: www.nfwbo.org

National Statistical Office of Mongolia
Urgamalsuvd Nanjid, Statistical Expert
P.O.B. #432
Ulaanbaatar-46
Mongolia
Telephone: 976-1-328780
            976-1-323943
Fax: 976-1-372865
      976-1-687313
Email: solo126@hotmail.com
        ur15@usa.net

New Economics Foundation
Andrew Simms, Campaign Leader
Cinnamon House
6-8 Cole Street
London SE1 4YH
UK
Telephone: 44-207-407-7447
Fax: 44-207-407-6473
E-mail: info@neweconomics.org
Website: www.neweconomics.org

Oxford Research Group
Scilla Elworthy, Director
51 Plantation Road
Oxford, OX2 6JE
UK
Telephone: 44-1865-242819
Email: org@oxfrg.demon.co.uk
Website: www.oxfrg.demon.co.uk

Peace Journalism, Conflict and Peace
Courses
Indra Adnan, Director
Annabel McGoldrick, Coordinator
Taplow Court, Taplow
Berkshire
England SL6 0ER
UK
Telephone: 44-1628-59-1239
Fax: 44-1628-77-3055
Email: conflict.peace@dartnet.co.uk

People-Centered Development Forum
David Korten
International Secretariat
14E 17th Street, Suite 5
New York 10003-1925
USA
Telephone: 206-842-0216
Fax: 212-242-1901

Email: pcdf@igc.org
Website: http://iisd1.iisd.ca/pcdf/

People's Forum 2001, Japan
Tomoko Sakuma, Director
Maruko Bldg. 3F
Higashi-ueno 1-20-6, Taito-ku
Tokyo
110-0015
Japan
Telephone: 813-3834-2436
Fax: 813-3834-2406
Email: tsakuma@jca.apc.org

Progressio Foundation
Marcello Palazzi, President
Parklaan 51
Doorn 3941 RD
The Netherlands
Telephone: 31-343-414-330
Fax: 31-343-420-030
Email: mpalazzi@compuserve.com

Promocion del Desarrollo Popular A.C.
Lopezliera Mendez Luis, President
Tialoc 40-3
Col. Anahuac 11370oDF
Mexico
Telephone: 52-5-535-0325
            52-5-566-4265
Fax: 52-5-592-1989
Email: espacios@laneta.apc.org

Public Citizen's Global Trade Watch
Lori Wallach, Director
215 Pennsylvania Avenue, SE
Washington, DC 20003
USA
Telephone: 202-546-4996
Fax: 202-547-7392
Email: lwallach@citizen.org
Website: www.tradewatch.org

Quaker United Nations Office
Lori Heninger, Associate
Representative
777 UN Plaza, 5ᵗʰ Floor
New York, NY 10017
USA
Telephone: 212-682-2745
Fax: 212-983-0034
Email: qunony@pipeline.com

Quantum Leap Project
1400 16ᵗʰ Street NW
Suite 501
Washington, DC 20008
Telephone: 202-797-6692

Fax: 202-797-5486
Email: buffet@nwf.org
Publishes via fax, *The Bull and the Bear*
newsletter on financial news for activists
and environmentalists.

Redefining Progress
1 Kearney St, 4th Floor
San Francisco Ca 94108
USA
Telephone: 415-781-1191
Fax: 415-781-1198
Email: info@rprogress.org
Website: www.rprogress.org

Right Livelihood Award Foundation
Jakob von Uexkull, Chairman
Box 15072
S-104 Stockholm
Sweden
Telephone: 46-8-702-0340
Fax: 46-8-702-0338
7 Park Crescent
London W1N 3HE
UK
Telephone: 44-207-404-5011
Fax: 44-207-433-1443

Santi Pracha Dhamma Institute
Sulak Sivaraska
113/115 Fuangnakhon Road
(opp. Wat Rajbopit)
Bangkok 10200
Thailand
Telephone: 662-223-4915
Fax: 662-225-9540
Email: atc@box1.a-net.net.th

Sarvodya Shramadana
Dr. A. T. Ariyaratne, President
98 Rawatawatta Road
Damsak, Mandira
Moratuwa
Sri Lanka
Telephone: 94-1-647-159
            94-1-645-255
Fax: 94-1-647-084

Society for International
Development (SID)
Tina Liamzon
Viale delle Terme di Caracala
Rome 00144
Italy
Telephone: 396-591-1145

Social Investment Forum, UK
Penny Shepherd, Director

Suite 308
16 Baldwin Gardens
London EC1N 7RJ
UK
Telephone: 44-207-404-1993
Fax: 44-207-404-1994
Email: info@uksif.org
Website: www.uksif.org

Social Investment Forum, US
Stephen Scheuth, President
1621 K Street NW, Suite 600
Washington, DC 20006
USA
Telephone: 202-872-5319
Fax: 202-331-8166

Social Venture Network
P.O. Box 29221
San Francisco, California 94129
USA
UK
Netherlands
Brazil
Thailand

Soka Gakkai International
Joan Anderson, Public Information Officer
15-3 Samon-cho, Shinjuku-ku
Toyko, 160-0017
Japan
Telephone: 81-3-5360-9831
Fax: 81-3-5360-9885
Email: jander@po.iijnet.or.jp

South Asia Watch on Trade
Economics and Development
Dhrubesh Chandra Regmi, Treasurer
P. B. No. 14307
Kathmandu
Nepal
Telephone: 977-1-490143
Fax: 977-1-493133
Email: fppi@sawtee.wlink.com.np

Susan George
10 rue Jean Michelez
Lardy
91510
France
Telephone: 33-1-6927-4715
Fax: 33-1-6082-6668
Email: susangeorge@wanadoo.fr

Third World Network
Martin Khor, Director
228 Macalister Road
Penang 10400

Malaysia
Telephone: 604-2266150
          604-2266159
Fax: 604-2264505
Email: twn@igc.apc.org
       twnpen@twn.po.my
Website: www.twns.ide.org.sg

Toda Institute
Dr. Majid Tehranian
Honolulu Center
Kapilani Blvd., Suite 1111
Honolulu, HI 96813
USA
Telephone: 808-955-8231
Fax: 808-955-6476
Email: mtehrani@isdi-hi.com

Trans National Institute
Fiona Dove
Paulus Potterstraat 20
Amsterdam
1071 DA
Netherlands
Telephone: 31-20-662-6608
Fax: 31-20-6757176
Email: fdove@worldcom.nl
Website: www.worldcom.nl/tni

UNCTAD
Carlos Fortin
Deputy Secretary-General, UNCTAD
Palais des Nations
Geneve 10, CH-1211
Switzerland
Telephone: 41-22-917-5809
          41-22-917-0042
Email: carlos.fortin@unctad.org

United Nations Volunteers
Postfach 260 111
D-53153
Bonn, Germany
Telephone: 49-228-8152000
Fax: 49-228-8152001
Email: hq@unv.org
Website: www.unv.org

UN Non-Governmental Liaison Service
(NGLS)
Hamish Jenkins, Programme Officer
Palais des Nations
Geneva
CH-1211
Switzerland
Telephone: 41-22-917-2078
Fax: 41-22-917-0049
Email: hamish.jenkins@unctad.org

Women's World Banking
Nancy Barry, President
140 East 40th Street
New York, NY 10016
USA
Telephone: 212-719-0414

World Federalist Movement,
International Secretariat
777 United Nations Plaza
New York, NY 10017
USA
Telephone: 212-599-1320
Fax: 212-599-1332
Email: wfm@igc.org
Website: www.worldfederalist.org

World Vision Australia
Brett Parris, Policy & Campaigns Officer
1 Vision Drive
East Burwood VIC
3151
Australia
Telephone: 61-3-9287-2383
Fax: 61-3-9287-2315
Email: parrisb@wva.org.au
Website: www.wvi.org/aus

World Wildlife Fund International
CH-1196 Gland
Switzerland
Telephone: 41-22-364-9111
Fax: 41-22-364-0074
Website: www.panda.org